ILR Paperback Number 18

WORKER PARTICIPATION AND OWNERSHIP

Cooperative Strategies for Strengthening Local Economies

William Foote Whyte

Tove Helland Hammer *Christopher B. Meek*

Reed Nelson *Robert N. Stern*

ILR PRESS
New York State School of
Industrial and Labor Relations
Cornell University
Ithica, NY 14853

Cover illustration and design: Kathleen King Whyte

Library of Congress number: 82-23413
ISBN: 0-87546-097-6

Cataloging in Publication Data

Main entry under title:

Worker participation and ownership.

(ILR paperback series ; 18)
Bibliography: p.
Includes index.
1. Employees' representation in management—United
States—Addresses, essays, lectures. 2. Employee
ownership—United States—Addresses, essays, lectures.
I. Whyte, William Foote, 1914–
HD5660.U5W67   1983   338.6   82-23413
ISBN 0-87546-097-6 (pbk.)

Copies may be ordered from

ILR Press
New York State School of
Industrial and Labor Relations
Cornell University
Ithaca, NY 14853

Printed in the United States of America

Contents

Foreword

America is on the threshold of economic change as significant as the Industrial Revolution in the last century. This transition will materially affect the organization of work, relationships between management and labor, economic development strategies, and, in some cases, the ownership of private business enterprises.

This incisive book represents a significant contribution to our understanding of some useful strategies to adapt this enormous change to our benefit. The combination of experience and analysis, or participative research, of the authors is crucial to the success and importance of this work.

A new style of labor-management relations can provide greater opportunity for economic progress, thereby contributing to the solution of the complex economic problems of the 1980s and beyond. The labor-management cooperative movement is struggling to achieve acceptance in what is still a very adversarial climate in this country. Leadership is vitally needed to define the mutual objectives of business and labor. It is often critical at the early stages of such an experience that competent third-party mediation be available to the parties.

Not only is labor-management cooperation a new style of employee relations, but it also presents us with a new culture in which to operate. This is a fundamental change from the adversarial culture of the past. It may even affect dispute resolution far removed from the area of labor-management relations. The institutionalization of labor-management committees represents an extremely important development in American society.

In order to successfully commence a cooperative venture, there must be a real commitment by the leaders on both sides so that common goals can be defined and progress can be achieved. It is very important to have patience in pursuing this commitment. Inevitably, there will be setbacks and periods of lull in the development of such a cooperative venture. It is also important to sustain the commitment and to not succumb to despair when these plateaus are reached.

It is very important to distinguish between labor-management cooperation at the workplace and employee investment in the reorganization of business enterprises. The first can occur in a variety of settings. It can be developed within an individual business; or it can involve an entire industry, such as the construction industry in a particular region; or it can involve the type of areawide committee formed in Jamestown, New York, whch is extensively discussed in this book. These ventures can proceed without ever affecting the nature of ownership in a business enterprise.

On the other hand, it occasionally occurs to areawide committees that the reorganization of a firm that might otherwise fail can be accomplished only with participation by the employees. Such ventures can serve as a useful component of an overall economic development strategy. This type of employee ownership can also occur with or without the prior development of a labor-management committee.

I unequivocally agree with the authors that employee ownership provides an effective option to many plant shutdowns and in many cases an effective overall strategy for local economic development. However, for employee ownership to be effective, it must be coupled with worker participation in the firm through labor-management cooperation or some type of quality of working life program. Without these vehicles for employee participation within the workplace, mere ownership can result in the confusion of purposes for both the manager and the production employees.

My own experience with this new form of cooperation and business organization came as a result of forming the Jamestown Area Labor-Management Committee about a decade ago. I have given an historical account of the development of that committee in a chapter in the recently published book *Managing Innovation: The Social Dimensions of Creativity, Invention and Technology*, edited by Sven Lundstedt and E. William Colglazier. The authors of the present book have now independently observed the innovation pioneered in Jamestown and very accurately assessed some of the lessons we learned. In the course of my experience as mayor of Jamestown, I became convinced that both workplace participation and employee ownership are extremely useful economic development techniques.

Since coming to the Congress, I have also had the opportunity to observe a number of different efforts across the country that attempted to forge a new partnership between labor and business and sometimes involved government as well. I have concluded that the entire nation could benefit from a reappraisal of some of the adversarial systems we have come to accept.

As the authors of this important work point out, the eventual solutions to many of our economic problems will be found at the local level. Nevertheless, state and federal governments can provide important support to facilitate the development of these innovative options. For example, I believe that it is critical that funding for the implementation of the Labor-Management Cooperation Act be increased to a much higher level than the Congess has been willing to appropriate in past years. Employee ownership initiatives could be more adequately supported by the U.S. Economic Development Administration. New forms of participative research could be supported by the federal government through the National Science Foundation and other institutions. The U.S. Department of Labor could provide more information to companies, unions, and local governments interested in this new cooperation. State governments could adopt various strategies to facilitate both labor-management cooperation and employee take-over of failing firms.

All these possibilities are given support and guidance by the work of the authors and Professor Whyte's Program on New Systems of Work and Participation. Many of the pitfalls of employee investment and worker participation are also described in this book. I am delighted that Cornell, which has provided important analysis of the collective bargaining process, now is also supporting the analysis of these methods of complementing the traditional method of allocating advances in productivity.

Representative Stan Lundine

Acknowledgments

THIS BOOK results from work done in Cornell University's New Systems of Work and Participation Program, which was begun in 1976 and was supported principally by grants from the Center for Work and Mental Health of the National Institute of Mental Health. A small grant from the U.S. Department of Labor helped to get the program started, and another grant from the department helped us write our research findings for practitioners in labor, management, and community affairs. Of course, the conclusions expressed here do not represent the views of the funding agencies.

We have benefited greatly from the field work, writings, and publications of former students: Michael Gurdon (on Saratoga Knitting Mill), Jeanette Eadon Johanneson (on Vermont Asbestos Group), Ana Gutiérrez-Johnson (on Mondragón), Richard Long (on Byers Transport Ltd.), Donna Sockell (on varoius cases), and Haydn Wood (on Mohawk Valley Community Corporation). For information, ideas, and critiques of earlier drafts, we are indebted to Joseph Blasi, Harvard University; Corey Rosen, National Center for Employee Ownership; and Warner Woodworth, Brigham Young University. Robert Keidel, Temple University, provided valuable criticisms and suggestions for the chapter on the Jamestown Area Labor-Management Committee. For our interpretation of the employee purchase of Hyatt-Clark Industries, we are indebted to Wynn Hausser, who also brought to our attention the Canadian model of government collaboration with management and labor in economic readjustment. For information on the union-management-government cooperative program in the clothing and textile industries, we are grateful to Jacob Sheinkman, secretary-treasurer to the Amalgamated Clothing and Textile Workers Union.

William Foote Whyte

1.
On the Need
for New Strategies

William Foote Whyte

THIS IS A TIME for rethinking industrial relations and economic development strategies. In the face of a severe recession and ballooning unemployment, there is a growing recognition that there are basic problems in our industrial relations and economic development strategies and that mere tinkering with the industrial machine will not recapture for the United States the industrial leadership we have been rapidly losing to Western Europe and particularly to Japan.

The Japanese challenge in key industries such as automotive, electronics, and steel has shattered the United States' complacency and provoked a frantic search for the secrets of Japan's success. It is ironic that Japan's industrial relations strategies have been based to some extent on ideas imported from the United States in the 1940s and 1950s. By the early 1940s, behavioral scientists here had discovered the potential benefits to morale and productivity of worker participation in decision making. In the immediate postwar era, Japanese industrial and governmental leaders and academicians, who realized that Japan's catastrophic military defeat required a rethinking of industrial relations and economic development strategies, eagerly reached out for new information and new ideas. Increasing numbers of Japanese visited the United States, and U.S. books and articles on human relations were translated into Japanese and widely read in that country. The Japanese were particularly interested in the writings of Douglas Magregor, Rensis Likert, Chris Argyris, and other exponents of participative management.

In 1951, W. Edwards Deming went to Japan to give lectures and workshops on modern statistical methods of quality control. Recognizing that before World War II Japanese exports had been viewed around the world as cheap but of low quality, the Japanese embraced the Deming methodology with enthusiasm, but they substantially transformed it to make it a basic element in a worker participation program. At the time, Deming thought he was teaching a methodology to be used by engineers and other management officials. It remained to the Japanese to discover possibilities of involving workers directly in the process of diagnosing problems of quality and production and of devising solutions to those problems. Robert Cole (1979) estimates that today one of every eight Japanese workers is involved in quality control circles during any year. Since the Japanese have had little success in extending quality control circles into commercial and service operations, this means that the kind of worker participation programs represented by quality control circles is particularly concentrated in manufacturing companies, whose products are in direct competition with U.S. producers.

While the ideology of worker participation was invented in the United States, in the early years these doctrines were taken much more seriously by Japanese than by U.S. management. In fact, Robert Cole explains the rapid spread of participation doctrines and practices in Japan as partly a response to what he calls a creative misunderstanding. When the Japanese read worker participation literature, many of them assumed that they were learning about programs and practices of the leading U.S. companies. Nothing could have been farther from the truth.

The basic obstacle to implementation of worker participation programs was that in the immediate postwar era U.S. management had unparalleled prestige all around the world. America was then known as the great arsenal of democracy. Even in the late 1960s, the French journalist Servan-Schreiber in his best-selling book *The American Challenge* (1968) argued that U.S. management methods were so far superior to those being practiced in Western Europe that the United States was in the process of taking over the European economy. There seemed no need to change what was apparently a winning game.

American executives are belatedly discovering that they are no longer playing a winning game and are having to rethink their basic assumptions and strategies. We hear ever more serious calls for the "reindustrialization of America." This book looks beyond such a slogan to examine several strategies that can make important contributions to American economic revival.

In searching for answers to problems of economic stagnation and high unemployment, the national political debate tends to center on what the federal government can and should do—or cannot or should not do. We have been seeking answers to a different question: What can local governments, community leaders, and labor and management officials do to revitalize local economies and to increase employment? We do not minimize the importance of federal policies and programs, and our final chapter considers changes at the national level that would stimulate and support local initiatives.

This new emphasis on local economies grows out of a reexamination of local development strategies. It is basically a shift from smokestack chasing to locally based and participatory strategies. Until recently, it was widely assumed that the way to solve the unemployment problem was to attract a big company into your community to build a new plant or to take over an abandoned plant. Experience is demonstrating the weaknesses of this strategy. It involves a wasteful use of local resources as many communities and states compete with each other to land a big plant from a big company; in this kind of a contest there is only one winner and a number of losers. Furthermore, in some cases the winners give up so much of their tax base to attract the company that they wonder later whether the victory was worth winning.

Another influence in reshaping economic development thinking has been the discovery of the fallacy of relying on big business to reduce unemployment. According to Representative John Breckenridge, reporting on a study by the House of Representatives Sub-Committee on Small Business, Anti-Trust, Consumers and Employment, in the eight years between 1969 and 1976, when total U.S. employment grew by more than 9.5 million jobs, the one thousand largest companies, which had provided over 20 percent of national employment in 1969, contributed less than 1 percent of the net increase in jobs (*Congressional Record* March 8, 1978). Another study (Birch 1979) has shown that firms with twenty or fewer employees accounted for over 50 percent of the net increase in the private sector jobs in the same eight-year period. In other words, the new jobs created by expansion of big companies tend to be offset by the jobs eliminated as companies invest in new equipment. While the employment potential of small business receives little public attention, experience and research are now showing that the greatest potential for job growth is in that sector of the economy.

The strategic implications of these findings are important. If local governments assume that economic growth and increasing employment in a local area come from initiatives of people in big business, backed up by the resources of their companies and banks and supported by professional expertise in management, production, and marketing, then these governments can contribute to economic growth only by cooperating with those companies. If, on the other hand, they recognize the enormous potential for job creation of small businesses, then it becomes apparent that the scope of the problems and the resources and expertise needed are much more within the capacity of local people.

This book does not attempt to provide a comprehensive treatment of all methods and policies that might be considered for saving jobs. It concentrates on what we have learned in the research carried out by Cornell University's New Systems of Work and Participation Program since 1976. Aside from one major project on the Basque worker industrial cooperatives in Spain (Gutiérrez-Johnson and Whyte 1977; Gutiérrez-Johnson 1982), we have been devoting our attention to the United States, focusing particularly upon two interrelated developments: labor-management cooperative problem-solving programs and the emergence of employee ownership as a means of saving jobs in the face of impending plant shutdowns.

In response to the challenges of foreign, and particularly Japanese, competition, there has been an explosive growth of participatory programs in a large number of major companies. Worker participation programs have also been spread by community-based organizations stimulating and guiding activity in a number of plants of different companies in their areas. Since our research has been concentrated on the Jamestown Area Labor-Management Committee since early 1976, chapters 2 and 3 describe and evaluate that model. Since the theoretical and practical conclusions drawn from the experience of the Jamestown committee can be usefully applied to programs within companies, we go beyond this particular case to explore some theoretical and practical implications.

The 1970s witnessed a sudden growth of employee and employee-community owned enterprises, and this movement continues to gain momentum in the 1980s. Chapter 4 presents what we have learned about the problems and processes of saving jobs through shifting ownership to workers and local people. The shift to employee ownership involves major changes in the role of the union, and chapter 5 analyzes these changes. Chapter 5 also provides an opportunity to link worker participation programs, as described in the Jamestown model, with employee ownership. Chapter 6 considers the policy options for union, management, and government leaders.

2.
Cooperative Problem Solving in Jamestown

Christopher B. Meek, Reed Nelson, and William Foote Whyte

IN THE WORLDWIDE quest for improvements in productivity and in the quality of working life in industry, Americans have created a distinctive social invention: the community or area labor-management committee. The Jamestown Area Labor-Management Committee (JALMC) is a potential model for other communities whose leaders are concerned with improving productivity and the quality of working life. This is not to suggest that Jamestown has achieved perfection in this field of rapidly growing public interest or that other communities should seek to follow Jamestown's example in every detail. We focus particularly on JALMC because it has gained a well-deserved national and international reputation as a successful program and because we have studied that program and also participated actively in it since 1976. Our involvement enables us not only to document the achievements of JALMC but also to distinguish between successful and unsuccessful local projects and thus analyze what it takes to develop and maintain such a community program (See also Keidel 1981a and 1981b; Meek 1983).

While area labor-management committees (LMCs) have a history of several decades, they are still much less familiar to students of industrial relations than union-management committees based in particular companies or individual factories. The company-based joint program has a much longer history and has enjoyed a sudden growth of interest among practitioners as well as among academicians because major companies and unions have sought to meet the Japanese challenge by developing their own styles of worker participation in decision making. We will not examine here the company-based programs currently in operation in General Motors, Ford Motor Company, Xerox Corporation, and elsewhere, but we should note that one of the major purposes of JALMC has been to provide stimulation and guidance for the formation and development of in-plant joint committees in the factories of Jamestown. Our examination of some of the in-plant programs in Jamestown will discuss problems and social processes similar to those encountered in individual company-based programs and will allow some conclusions on union-management cooperation at the plant or company level as well as in the community or area.

The first area LMC was founded in Toledo, Ohio, after World War II. Actually, a local body had existed since 1936 when the city council established the Toledo Industrial Peace Board, which anticipated later LMCs in its structure. It was composed of five representatives from management, five from the unions, and eight from the public sector. During the war, the National War Labor Board took over the Industrial Peace Board's functions (Foltman 1976). The present Toledo Labor-Management-Citizens Committee was formed in 1945 through the efforts of the vice mayor and a local attorney (Blondman 1978). The purview of the new committee was expanded beyond mediation to include other issues such as recruitment of new industry, patronage of local industrial products, and educational efforts. Its major emphasis has continued to be prevention of strikes through locally based mediation.

In 1946 Louisville, Kentucky, followed Toledo's example in forming an area LMC. As in Toledo, the municipal government provided the catalyst to bring labor and management representatives together. The committee began as an informal group initiated by the mayor and was formally established and funded by the city council in late 1947. As in Toledo, the main activity of the Louisville committee was local mediation and arbitration of labor disputes.

The 1970s witnessed a new and broader wave in the development of area or community LMCs, with the latest count showing more than twenty such organizations in existence. This new wave is of interest not only because of the much larger number of communities involved but also because of a general shift in emphasis. As federal and state mediation services filled the gap noted in Toledo and Louisville in the immediate postwar period, the area LMCs of the 1970s directed increasing attention to projects designed to improve productivity and the quality of working life.

The Jamestown program presents these distinctive features:

1. Cooperative action by labor, management, and local government to save jobs in plant shutdowns and to strengthen the economic base of the community

2. Creation of in-plant cooperative problem-solving projects in which labor and management jointly define, examine, and make decisions about problems, with JALMC staff members playing facilitating roles

3. Training local management and union people to take over this facilitating role in their own firm or in other local companies

4. Organizing communitywide training programs to strengthen the skills base needed by local industry

5. Developing joint projects with other community organizations such as the Chautauqua County Industrial Development Agency, the Jamestown school system, and the Jamestown Community College.

6. Avoiding involvement in the mediation of labor-management conflicts.

The decision to avoid the mediating role required JALMC to discover new ways of helping the parties and the city to solve their problems.

Before the founding of JALMC, Jamestown had experienced a long and severe economic decline. An industrial city with a population of about forty thousand in a metropolitan area totaling sixty thousand, Jamestown had about twice the proportion of manufacturing employment to total employment as the average city in New York State.

Industry in Jamestown has been heavily concentrated in furniture and metal shops, and the furniture industry especially had been losing ground for decades. At the beginning of the century, there were thirty-four plants manufacturing wood furniture, and by 1972 the number had dropped to fourteen. While the drop in the wood furniture industry had been most drastic, employment figures for Jamestown's manufacturing industries as a whole show a steady decline for the eighteen years before 1972.

The labor force in Jamestown was highly unionized. Over the years Jamestown had been unable to attract new industry because of its reputation for having a bad labor climate. In the years preceding the formation of JALMC, increasing severity of strikes was associated with the shift in ownership to outside interests. While the frequency of strikes was only slightly higher in the absentee-owned firms, there was an enormous difference in strike duration: the average strike in a locally owned firm was settled in 8.7 days compared with 40.0 days in the plants owned by outsiders (Meek 1983). The growth of absentee ownership was clearly making it more difficult for Jamestown people to resolve labor conflicts.

Growing public awareness of Jamestown's problems led in the early 1960s to the first tentative efforts to cope with labor problems in manufacturing plants. A still earlier and continuing experience with a union-management committee in the construction industry suggested the possibility of building a similar joint organization in manufacturing.

A local labor attorney, Ray Anderson, began consulting with Sam Sackman of the Federal Mediation and Conciliation Service and with Al Mardin, executive director of the Jamestown Area Manufacturers Association . They believed that the Toledo labor-management committee had been successful in changing the image of that city from a "bad labor town" and thought something along that line might fit the needs in Jamestown. Both Anderson and Sackman had had experience with company-based LMCs elsewhere and helped start several in-plant committees in Jamestown in the late 1960s and early 1970s. Their project, however, could not get off the ground without the leadership of the mayor of Jamestown.

ORGANIZING THE RESPONSE TO THE COMMUNITY CRISIS: 1971–73

The chronic problems of Jamestown suddenly became acute in 1971 with the announcement of the closing of the Art Metal Plant. This was an especially severe blow since the company had been in that area for seventy years and had been the largest employer, with as many as seventeen hundred on the payroll at times. Furthermore, the company was abandoning a virtually new one million–square-foot plant. But even the Art Metal shutdown was not the end of the threatened decline. Jamestown faced the possibility of imminent closings of six more plants, which would bring the total loss of employment to thirty-five hundred jobs.

In this crisis, Anderson, Sackman, and Mardin met with Sam Nalbone, the city ombudsman, who had formerly been a business agent for the International Association of Machinists and Aerospace Workers. Nalbone brought them together with Stanley Lundine, who had been elected mayor in 1970. This was a case of the right man being in the right place at the right time. Proponents of the LMC idea saw in the city government a neutral institution concerned with the overall economic interests of the community. Lundine had come into office already enjoying a measure of confidence from leaders of labor and management. His family had roots in both camps. An uncle on his mother's side had been a national leader with the IAM, and his father was the owner-manager of one of the Jamestown manufacturing companies. Lundine had received strong political backing from both groups. John Walker, a prominent local manager, had organized Republicans for Lundine and had been able to gain the endorsement of a number of manufacturing and business leaders. The project naturally appealed to a man who had campaigned for an activist city government committed to solving the critical social and economic problems of the community.

Lundine had already discovered that traditional development strategies would not work for Jamestown. As he said several years later,

> I had thought, I guess with some degree of naïveté, that we could just go out and lure industry into this area, and that all we needed was an industrial development program. I went all over seeking new industry for the area, and it seemed that everywhere I went they said that we had a bad

labor climate. . . . So I decided that redevelopment in the conventional sense just wasn't enough for us. We had to plunge into the economic area. Having decided that, it's pretty obvious that Jamestown is a manufacturing town. . . . Having analyzed the manufacturing, it was very obvious we had a highly unionized town. So I felt that you had to get the top executives of the manufacturing companies and the union leaders to talk about their problems. No government program was essentially going to solve it.

Assisted by Anderson, Sackman, and Mardin, Lundine took the initiative. He met first with key leaders of labor and management separately and then brought the two groups together. The first joint meeting in February 1972 began stormily. Labor people accused management of keeping new business out of town in order to keep wages low, and management, while ridiculing that charge, accused labor leaders of causing the bad labor climate. After the charges and countercharges had been vented Lundine got the parties talking about what might be done to improve this situation:

We agreed temporarily that there would be a committee, the labor-management committee, we would not form it legally, and it would not have a separate identity, it would be the type of thing where anybody could take a walk anytime they wanted to. We agreed that at the next meeting we would choose co-chairmen.

In the March meeting, after a good deal of informal consultation with leaders of both parties, Lundine got the joint group together once more to choose cochairmen: for labor, Joe Mason, business agent for the IAM; for management, Skip Yahn, plant manager at the American Sterilizer Company plant. The group also agreed on four objectives: improvement of area labor relations, manpower development, assistance to local industrial development, and improving productivity through cooperative effort.

The commitment of labor to productivity required a good deal of consultation and conversation outside the meetings. Labor leaders were naturally suspicious of an objective that might mean speedup and loss of jobs. A key premeeting discussion between Lundine and Joe Mason ended with this statement by the labor leader, as recalled by Lundine:

"Okay, productivity becomes a major objective, but—one, we want an understanding that it's not going to be used to cut out workers. If we're going to improve productivity in a plant, then management is going to do everything possible not to lay off workers. Two, we want a general sort of understanding, without any sort of negotiating up front, that gains would be shared equally by labor and management, and three, we want to define it broadly, we don't want speedup." Now those weren't all Joe's ideas; those were ideas that kind of developed in those side meetings. On that basis Joe was willing to accept the co-chairmanship.

The March meeting also led to an agreement on ground rules: membership on the committee was to be entirely voluntary, and there would be a balance between labor and management both for cochairmen and for the total membership. JALMC would avoid any direct involvement in collective bargaining except for possible development of labor relations courses or workshops. The committee would also avoid any involvement in mediation of labor disputes. (For an account of this formative period, see Lundine 1982).

The ban on the mediation role was urged particularly by Sackman. He argued that there was no need to duplicate the programs of the Federal Mediation and Conciliation Service or the New York State Mediation Service. While this might be interpreted as simply a defense of the turf of FMCS and its sister state agency, this decision was essential in opening the field for innovative lines of development. If JALMC had assumed responsibility for mediation, this would have led the committee so deeply into the collective bargaining process as to rule out other lines of development.

The mayor and the city ombudsman were accepted as ex-officio members of the committee. Their ex-officio status underlined their commitment to placing decision making in the hands of the labor and management members, while at the same time placing them in strategic positions to carry out the behind-the-scenes work of keeping the parties together.

The first order of business was to stave off the shutdown of Chautauqua Hardware, which would have meant the loss of three hundred jobs. This was an old, locally owned firm, which had been seriously mismanaged, and productivity per worker there was only about 60 percent of the industrywide average. The mayor and the local union leaders joined to persuade the bankruptcy court to allow the plant to keep operating in the hopes that new management and new investment money could be brought in to fend off the sale of equipment to a liquidator. With advice and assistance from other members of the committe, the mayor went about finding potential investors and managers. Since such new people were not inclined to put up money and assume management responsibilities without prospects of improvement in labor relations and productivity, the mayor got the potential new owner-managers together with the local union leaders to reach an understanding on future cooperative efforts.

In bargaining the first contract in the fall of 1972, management negotiators announced that their unconditional offer had to be limited to a 4 percent cost of living adjustment but that if the union would work with them to bring the company up to or above the industry average in productivity per worker, substantial productivity bonuses could be paid. The parties then negotiated the formula for such payments, thus signing Jamestown's first productivity agreement.

Except that no explicit productivity agreements were reached in other threatened shutdowns, the mayor and committee members followed a similar pattern of personal contact, persuading, and assisting in securing financing. In the period beginning with Chautauqua Hardware in June 1972 to February 1974, JALMC was successful in five of six efforts to forestall shutdowns, thus saving 756 jobs. In three of the cases, the ownership shift was from a conglomerate to local owner-managers. In the Chautauqua Hardware case, the shift was from a local owner-manager group to outside owner-managers, who then settled in Jamestown. In the case of Jamestown Metal Products, the shift was from conglomerate ownership to employee ownership.

This was the period of intense activity by the mayor and key members of the labor-management committee, with the minimal staff assistance that could be afforded on the locally available funds. Committee members were keenly aware of the need to gain outside financing, and they had prepared a funding proposal for government agencies in Washington as early as the spring of 1972. Accompanied by Joe Mason and Wally Dixon, a management member from American Voting Machine, Lundine made the rounds of various agencies, without success. He reported that the general reaction was that Jamestown had something very interesting and valuable, "but we don't have a program to fit it." Early in 1973, the Economic Development Administration (EDA) discovered a potential program fit. Robert Jackson invited Lundine to come back to Washington and work out the financing arrangements. There followed a much smaller grant from the National Center on Productivity and Quality of Working Life.

It was not until the late spring of 1973 that JALMC could begin to build a professional staff, and, to the end of this period of development, that staff was limited to James McDonnell, who took a leave of absence from Buffalo State College to work with JALMC full time. While McDonnell had little involvement in the crisis efforts to prevent plant shutdowns, he concentrated on the less dramatic but important function of developing in-plant committees to work on productivity and the quality of working life. McDonnell also established the annual summer JALMC steak fry. This was important symbolically for bringing together leaders of labor and management to eat and drink, to reach out personally beyond the traditional adversary relationship.

This period brought the first fruits of the campaign to attract new industry into Jamestown. In June 1974, Cummins Engine Company announced that it was taking over the abandoned Art Metal plant, with the expectation that its local employment would reach fifteen hundred in the 1980s. Cummins officials let it be known that the improved labor climate growing out of JALMC activities had been a major factor in their decision to locate a major facility in Jamestown. Besides this boost to local pride, Jamestown gained an employer known for its imaginative approach to job redesign and quality of working life and productivity projects, thus significantly adding to the leadership available within management for JALMC.

IN-PLANT AND COMMUNITY PROBLEM SOLVING PROJECTS, 1974–77

Eric Trist entered the Jamestown program in May of 1973, but the funds available at the time provided only for a diagnostic effort that could be carried out by Trist and his associates on the basis of occasional visits for plant tours and discussions with labor, management, and community officials. These visits provided an orientation to the local scene and an opportunity to develop strategic plans, but the projects themselves could not be developed until JALMC received further funding from EDA, which made it possible to bring John Eldred and Robert Keidel to Jamestown on a full-time basis, in addition to the continuing visits by Trist.

The involvement of Trist brought to Jamestown the diagnostic skills and strategic ideas of one of the most eminent behavioral scientists in industrial relations. Starting action research in the late 1940s with the Tavistock Institute in England, Trist developed his strategy of dealing with industrial and business firms as sociotechnical systems. This meant viewing the problem of improving organizational performance and the quality of working life through redesigning both the social system and the technological system. Before coming to the United States and eventually to the Wharton School at the University of Pennsylvania, Trist had stimulated innovative strategies for the improvement of productivity and quality of working life in Scandinavian and other countries.

Trist's diagnostic studies revealed a key communitywide problem: the impending loss of the base of skilled workers in the furniture industry. Over the years, as employment had declined, the only skilled men remaining in the plants were in their fifties and sixties. In fact, the problem was already so acute in some plants that the absence of one skilled worker might cause a shutdown of a whole department.

To follow up on the Trist diagnosis, McDonnell organized Jamestown's first industrywide training program, linking Jamestown Community College with the United Furniture Workers Union of America and the Jamestown Manufacturers Association. The skilled workers knew nothing about teaching, and the college teachers knew nothing about woodworking skills, but pairs of teachers and skilled craftsmen worked together on a highly successful program that drew students from many of the firms. Financing was provided by the Chautauqua County Industrial Development Agency.

By the time Eldred and Keidel settled in Jamestown in the late spring of 1975, James Schmatz had succeeded McDonnell as coordinator. The staff also included a local man, Tony Prinzi. The new outside staff members were greeted by the members of management and labor with considerable reserve. Management particularly was skeptical about the potential of university people to help Jamestown.

Jamestown presented Trist and his associates with a type of technology that had received very little attention in industrial relations research. Most of the plants in Jamestown are job shops that produce custom items one unit at a time or in small batches. They produce a wide variety of items, which require frequent and difficult adjustments. In large manufacturing or mass production operations, the problem of consultants in improving the quality of working life is to break into the rigidities of mass production and introduce more flexibility and adaptability. In Jamestown there seemed to be the opposite problem: one of decreasing chaos rather than increasing variety. Most plants operated with small margins and could not afford to hire staff to work on complex organizational and production problems.

Conditions in Jamestown favored the development of a cooperative problem-solving strategy. Some of the firms were in such a precarious economic condition that management and union leaders had to seek improvements through new methods. Furthermore, key management people, unlike their predecessors of earlier decades, had not worked their way up through the shop and so lacked the intimate knowledge of shop conditions, processes, and problems that would have enabled them to make their own decisions without consultation.

Eldred and Keidel worked in ten different companies, seeking to start labor-management committees in some of them and to strengthen existing committees. In one case, management abandoned participation before the project was well underway, and in another case, the union leadership pulled out—but only after one success had been achieved. In two cases, the consultants decided to withdraw when the projects appeared to be bogging down and there was not sufficient union or management support to warrant continued effort. JALMC did, however, achieve some notable successes that helped to build the credibility of the program locally and to stir interest among outside observers.

Eldred began working with union and management at Carborundum when top management was planning to redesign and expand what had become a very old and inefficient plant. In October 1975, management contracted with a consulting engineering firm for the redesign of the plant, and at the same time the plant labor-management committee formed a subcommittee on plant layout. The subcommittee designed a survey, which would be administered by the supervisors, to canvass all workers for ideas and information. Management intended for the subcommittee to collaborate with the engineering firm, but the engineers saw no need for collaboration.

In April 1976, the consultants presented management with a proposal calling for an investment of between $9 million and $10 million. The plant engineer characterized the proposal: "It gave what they thought we wanted but not what we needed. . . . It was an engineer's dream and a production man's nightmare."

Rejecting the consultant's plan, management now turned the problem over to the LMC subcommittee. The survey had brought in 172 concrete ideas, and the subcommittee used, to some degree, about 75 percent of these along with the consultants' proposal to work out two alternative plans of its own. In August 1976, the labor-management committee gave these plans to local and divisional managers for detailed studies of costs and potential savings.

In April 1977, the president and vice president of the company visited Jamestown to tour the plant and to review the redesign plans. Labor members of the LMC took the lead in explaining and selling the plan. They regarded it as a victory for labor when top management approved the plan and authorized a project that eventually cost $5.8 million. Since an old and inefficient plant is likely to be shut down in a future recession, this major modernization project meant greatly increased job security. It also involved exchanging cramped and dingy locker rooms for more spacious modern facilities.

For management, the cooperative project produced a rebuilt plant judged to be far more efficient than that projected by the consultants—at a savings of more than $3 million. For the city of Jamestown, this meant a strengthened tax base, with the prospect of future expansion in business and jobs. The groundbreaking in August 1977 became a community ceremonial event and brought together labor and management with city officials, along with former mayor and Representative Lundine.

In 1976 JALMC set a new course with the development of an autonomous work group or self-managing team in one department of American Sterilizer Company (AMSCO). In December 1975, AMSCO plant manager Jim Laughner explained to John Eldred and the plant's labor-management committee that the introduction of new machinery into the sink polishing department would mean loss of twenty jobs unless other work could be found. In response to this announcement, Eldred suggested the formation of a self-managing work team within the department. Its goal would be to increase productivity and to expand the duties of workers so that every worker would be capable of doing all jobs, including some supervisory functions typically handled by management. Willing to try anything that might protect the jobs, the union members of the in-plant committee accepted the idea, and Laughner promised management support.

In January 1976, the plan was taken directly to the members of the polishing department, and sixteen of the department's eighteen employees enthusiastically volunteered to participate. The following month was spent developing a formal project proposal and gaining full union support. The self-managing team was initiated in March, at which time the LMC agreed that the project would be given a six-month test period.

As the months passed, the polishing department substantially improved its performance in terms of productivity and product quality. Turnover ceased—a great surprise since the polishing department was considered one of the most undesirable work areas because of its dirty working conditions and heavy physical demands. All but one of the team's original sixteen members became committed to the effort, and even the two holdouts, older workers, decided to join the group. Positive changes were also reflected when new labor-management projects made requests for volunteers; polishing department members applied for literally all new projects. Several team members who had previously been notorious for filing grievances and hassling the foreman made complete turnarounds and focused their energies on suggesting a variety of ways to improve departmental and plant performance.

In short, the polishing department was turned on by this experience with self-management.

The AMSCO LMC was also the first to tackle cooperative job costing. In March 1976, plant manager Laughner received a memo from the corporation's home office announcing that the company was willing to manufacture a number of products that had previously been contracted for. Enclosed was a list of twenty-five items. The memo indicated that any of the firm's plants could make any one of the items if it could produce the item at a lower cost than their outside or internal competitors. The Jamestown plant had a short time to prepare bids, and it was apparent that bidding on even one of the items would severely strain the local management and industrial engineering staff. Eldred suggested that the plant manager pick one item on which to bid and then involve the LMC in the project. Laughner described the beginning of the project:

> We needed work pretty badly. Our market was starting to drop off. I was afraid that our costs were going up. So I took a look around this corporation for a product that we could do here, and I found one that was being made for our area facility but being produced by a vendor. I went to the union and told them that what I would like them to do is take a look at these charts—there was about a million and a half dollars worth of sales in there—and have them give me a quote for the corporation. And if the quote was equal to or better than the existing costs then I'd get the product for them. So what we did was ask for six volunteers from the factory to work as industrial engineers for whatever period was required to complete that piece of work. I took one of my most astute I.E. people and put him in a room with them, and we taught them what they needed to know in order to do this piece of work. How to put the weldings on a piece of paper, what the machine numbers were. In the area of standards, which we had to have, we gave them permission to go out on the floor to their peers to ask questions and query how long it would take.

The six-person task force worked throughout the month of April on a complete package of material and labor estimates for the potential new in-house product called the transfer loading car, a stainless steel metal cabinet on wheels used for delivering meals in hospitals. Several members of the sink polishing department's self-managing work team worked on this project along with workers from other parts of the plant. This group moved back and forth, collecting information from their fellow employees and vendors and then analyzing and compiling it. Laughner gave his impression of their progress:

> What happened was those guys were so energetic. . . . I'm telling you that I couldn't stay out of that conference room and getting myself involved after I saw the way they were working. I'd go in there and they'd be talking, and I'd see them go down to get a cup of coffee down past my office and they weren't talking about last night's Buffalo Bills game, they were talking about the damn car. In fact, I really realized how serious they were about the project when a very funny incident took place. One day when I popped my head in the door and one guy started to say, "That S.O.B. . . . ," and then they saw me and he shut up and didn't say anything more. So I said, "Ah, come on now, you can say anything in front of me. What were you talking about?" So the guy said, "I was out in the welding area, and I asked this one guy what the standard was for a certain job and he gave me a bad standard. So I asked him a second time in a different way and then two more times after that. He was still giving me a bad standard and I knew it. I finally got pretty frustrated and said, "Is that the proper standard?" He still insisted it was, so what I started to say when you came in was, "If that S.O.B. doesn't care about bringing this work into the shop, we're just gonna have to contract it out!"
>
> That really surprised me. You know if you want to get into a real pow-wow with the union all you have to do is start talking about subcontracting out work. You'll have a pretty terrible thing on your hands. But they were really seeing how that can happen at that time. I think that project was really a high point in our whole labor-management program.

By the end of April, the job-costing task force had completed the project, submitting documents to Laughner supporting a price bid to beat the competition. The transfer loading car then became a permanent part of the plant's production for at least three years. This meant a 15 percent cost savings to the corporation, and forty employees escaped layoff because of the $1.5 million in new business annually. The success of the transfer loading car project encouraged the plant LMC to go on to other successful cooperative job-costing projects.

Like many Jamestown firms, Hopes Windows secured a large portion of its business on the basis of competitive bids. When the bids on more complex projects were put together in the traditional fashion by members of management alone, Hopes was successful in only one out of ten cases. Furthermore, the company was losing money when some of its bids were lower than the eventual costs of production. When, with the assistance of Robert Keidel and Larry Carter, a professor at Jamestown Community College, the parties set up committees of workers, union officers, foremen, and engineers to work together on preparing bids, Hopes raised its success ratio to five out of ten. This was not simply a matter of workers revealing to management what they already knew about the problems and possibilities of doing their jobs. Workers came to understand costs, and they developed cost-saving ideas that would not have occurred to them before their participation on these committees. Their involvement also led them to recognize the importance of cost efficiency in protecting and expanding employment. Earlier, when work was slack, workers had a tendency to slow down so that they would not run out of work and be laid off.

In 1976, JALMC became involved with the Jamestown school system. John Sember, a junior high school teacher invited Eldred to speak to one of his classes. Eldred and Sember then cooperated on the development of an eight-week teaching module on industrial relations, productivity, and the quality of working life. Extending what JALMC was learning about cooperative problem solving in industry to the younger generation helped to narrow the gap between school and industry.

Nineteen seventy-seven marked the renewal of community-wide skills training in woodworking, which now became institutionalized with an industrywide joint committee to assess needs and plan programs. From 1975 through 1979, 2,415 workers were trained at a cost of $29.75 per worker.

As a means of building consultant skills into the community, JALMC organized a cadre training program. Seventeen trainees participated, nine from the unions, eight from management. This program began with a weekend seminar and continued with day-long meetings every two weeks, with the companies and unions paying for time off from regular jobs. As part of the program, trainees accompanied staff members for work on projects in plants where they were not employed.

As Jamestown began attracting a growing number of national and international visitors, JALMC sought to meet a growing demand for information and at the same time to protect its staff from the demands of telling the Jamestown story again and again. At this writing, JALMC has produced video tapes on the Carborundum redesign project, the Hopes Windows product bidding project, and the wood skills training program.

Toward the end of this period, Robert Keidel and John Eldred left JALMC. Chris Meek was to remain in Jamestown until June 1981, which meant that Cornell University was becoming the primary university link for JALMC.

GROWING INSTITUTIONALIZATION, 1977–82

By 1977, JALMC had become widely known throughout the industrial world, and yet the program in Jamestown was in a precarious situation. From December 1978 into June 1979, JALMC struggled with a financial crisis that threatened its existence. EDA had been the main source of funds in the early years but could not justify long-term funding of a local program.

The committee itself was now suffering from the informality and flexibility of procedures that had been so advantageous in the beginning. The only part of the structure and procedures that had been specified was that there should be labor and management cochairpersons and that the committee should strive to maintain a labor-management balance in its total membership. Subcommittees created at the outset had become inactive, and the executive committee's responsibilities could hardly be discharged by a body of fifteen to twenty members. Furthermore, there had been no provision for rotation of leadership position, which made for problems if a cochairperson became inactive. This kind of loose structure was viable in the early years because it was the staff members who ran the program. They consulted committee members from time to time and called executive committee meetings at irregular intervals, generally using these meetings to report on progress and gain the continuing endorsement of the members. The financial crisis from

December 1978 to June 1979 served the purpose of precipitating a reorganization of program and structure. The crisis was aggravated, furthermore, by the need to change coordinators at the same time the executive committee struggled to strenthen the financial position and gain a more active role in shaping the program. The executive committee agreed on a reduced budget and staff and appointed a coordinator for a year.

With the executive board and the staff now working closely together, JALMC secured a final grant of $36,900 from EDA and a $40,000 grant from the Appalachian Regional Commission, through New York State. The Chautauqua County Industrial Development Agency provided $19,000. Mayor Steven Carlson pledged that the city of Jamestown would continue its annual appropriation of $35,000. Management people from local companies promised to try to match that amount. Recognizing that it would be impossible for their members to match company contributions, the union leaders nevertheless pledged an active campaign to raise local money.

JALMC moved on from the financial crisis to reorganize its structure and procedures. A subcommittee wrote and gained acceptance for a constitution and bylaws that, among other things, established fixed periods of office of cochairpersons and also for labor and management members of the committee. The goal of this was to provide for rotation of leadership through JALMC in future years. The committee also established two permanent subcommittees, one on programs and the other on financing, so that it would be possible for the coordinator and staff members to work closely with the labor-management leadership in both these important fields rather than having the staff carry nearly all the responsibilities.

Besides the increased activity of the executive board, self-sufficiency in staff and in-plant activities increased. Skills upgrading was integrated with the activities of the local Private Industry Council, which brought the program more into the mainstream of community affairs and strengthened its financial base.

Perhaps more significant was the development of more autonomous in-plant efforts. Because of the unfamiliar nature of in-plant LMC activities, outside consultants had earlier taken the lead in organizing and directing in-plant committees. Then in 1979, a local graduate of the cadre program, Richard Walker, was loaned for eighteen months to JALMC by Cummins Engine. Working with Meek, Walker became an effective consultant and assumed direction of in-plant projects when Meek left in 1981. Walker was Jamestown's first locally trained full-time consultant, but unfortunately he was killed in an automobile accident a few months later.

During the same period, one of the committee's founders, city ombudsman Sam Nalbone, became coordinator. Thus, JALMC had gone from a period of heavy outside guidance to local leadership. Contacts with outside organizations remain, but the emphasis is now on development of local consulting talent. In 1981, the FMCS granted JALMC $73,753 specifically for further training and development of local part-time third parties to service Jamestown in-plant LMCs. The experience of several consultants who have worked in Jamestown has been recorded in videotapes and other training materials which JALMC uses in developing local staff.

The foundation of this new self-sufficiency lies in an approach to LMC facilitation that gradually emerged and was further developed by Meek and Walker: In some of the early cases, the plant-wide LMC had become dormant. The staff member then worked closely with a joint task force especially selected for a particular project. While it might have been necessary in the early period when staff members felt under great pressure to demonstrate the benefits of particular projects, this strategy provided for no continuity from project to project. Furthermore, when a given project bogged down, as some inevitably did, the lack of a joint plantwide committee deprived a task force of the support and guidance that might have been obtained from a committee with responsibility for planning, monitoring, and guiding its efforts. Meek and Walker insisted that any firm entering into a cooperative project set up such a joint plantwide steering committee.

When such projects were still unfamiliar to labor and management participants, the staff member had tended to assume the role of moderator and discussion leader. This active leadership role by the third party may have been necessary in getting the first projects moving, but it had the disadvantage of maintaining dependence of the parties upon the staff person. If he was not available, committees usually did not meet, and they looked to the third party to resolve problems when their efforts bogged down. This meant that the staff member was severely limited in the number of cases in which he could serve as a third party. Now, although the staff member may agree to conduct the first meetings in which the parties are considering whether they want to establish a plant labor-management committee, he proceeds only when the parties are able to agree that they will themselves take over leadership of the meetings. In the new pattern, labor and management representatives, who are appointed as cochairpersons by their groups, alternate between taking minutes and chairing the meeting. The consultant's role has become one of sitting in on meetings when possible, observing the process and offering suggestions and criticisms, but always seeking to encourage a process that will continue in his or her absence.

This new approach to third-party consultation grew out of a program at Corry-Jamestown Company that began in 1976 after a bitter nine-week strike. This plant of approximately five hundred workers manufactures high-quality metal office furniture and is located in Corry, Pennsylvania, a small city about twenty-five miles southwest of Jamestown. Corry's involvement began at the invitation of JALMC's labor cochairman, Joe Mason, whose IAM responsibilities included representing workers in this plant.

Because of the company's distance from Jamestown, JALMC coordinator Jim Schmatz worked out an approach that would enable him to sit in on committee meetings on a limited basis. This resulted in the formation of a steering or umbrella committee, led jointly by union and management, which spun off various problem-solving projects to be tackled by subcommittees.

The Corry-Jamestown committee undertook a number of joint projects, many of which were quite successful, but the first major undertaking involved the implementation of a cost-reduction–gains-sharing program. For this project, management brought in an outside consultant, Mitchell Fein, creator of the Impro-Share program. By this time Chris Meek and Patrick McGinity, staff consultant from the Wharton School, had assumed the third-party role at Corry-Jamestown. They worked closely with labor and management to structure the process of introducing the plan, so as to ensure that it was jointly implemented and that all workers had full opportunity to express their concerns as well as to gain a basic understanding of the new program. Management estimates that, compared with preplan performance, productivity was up by nearly 17 percent in 1978, by 18 percent in 1979, by 17 percent in 1980, and by about 12 percent in 1981. This meant worker bonuses of 6 to 9 percent of wages annually during this four-year period.

Encouraged by the success of this joint effort, management and labor worked together on a program in which worker participation in problem solving has become fully integrated into the process of managing the plant. This new managerial style involved so many meetings of the steering committee, of department committees, and of special task forces, that Meek and McGinity could attend only a few of them, but they continued to keep in close touch with union and management leaders, discussing overall strategy with them. The labor-management committee at Corry-Jamestown has moved beyond solving immediate problems to anticipating future problems and opportunities through joint long-range planning.

This institutionalization has also been characterized by the increasingly conscious transmission of the learning process from one company to another within the greater Jamestown area. The foundation for increased interorganizational learning had been laid earlier by JALMC's annual conferences, which brought together local management and labor people with interested outsiders, and by the formal teaching activities of Eldred and Keidel, such as a seminar on gains sharing in 1977. These activities prompted interorganizational visiting by management and labor people to compare experiences and ideas. Corry-Jamestown people, for example, discussed Impro-Share with Carborundum people, and, likewise, labor and management members of the Carborundum redesign subcommittee assisted a similar group at Corry-Jamestown in planning a major plant restructuring project.

When Dahlstrom Manufacturing Company labor and management became interested in gains sharing, Corry's orientation was influential in the formation of the program. In turn, Dahlstrom personnel have provided information on their experience to Hopes Windows, which is currently considering some kind of gains sharing. Hopes shared its experience with cooperative labor-management product bidding with the Watson Industries LMC and other firms in the area. The Watson LMC also toured the facilities of Weber Knapp Corporation in connection with a project considering new options for die storage. A committee at Fairbank Farms met with the new employee orientation subcommittee of the Carborundum LMC to tap its experience. The effects of these direct meetings have been multiplied through presentations of in-plant committees at JALMC conferences and dinners. These exchanges of information and ideas have been important in stimulating a climate of innovation and cooperation among Jamestown area firms.

COSTS AND BENEFITS

It is impossible to provide a complete record of costs and benefits of JALMC, but a rough accounting is within reach. It is, of course, easier to measure dollars spent directly by JALMC, and we shall make no effort to measure the value of the time contributed to the program by many community members. Table 1 reports on the financial support secured by JALMC for the ten years following its creation in the early spring of 1972.

The Wharton School of the University of Pennsylvania and Cornell University contributed professional services, but the costs of these activities could just as well be charged to the advancement of research and the enrichment of teaching at the universities, since involvement with JALMC continues to lead to theses, publications, and teaching materials. In general, the various companies did not keep records to allocate costs for the time management and labor devoted to in-plant LMCs, but it must be assumed that in the view of the decision makers the benefits of these activities at least equaled their costs.

The most dramatic and easily measurable benefits are found in the jobs saved through avoidance of plant shutdowns. Furthermore, the job benefits cannot be calculated simply in terms of the level of employment at the time of impending shutdown since, as table 2 indicates, five of the six firms saved recorded moderate to

TABLE 1. Financial Support of JALMC, 1972–81

Economic Development Administration	$470,000
City of Jamestown	267,000
Chautauqua County Industrial Development Agency	94,100
National Manpower Institute	60,000
Appalachian Regional Commission (through New York State)	40,000
Total	$931,100

TABLE 2. Employment Saved and Added as a Result of JALMC

Company	Employment at Closing	Employment as of June 1981
Chautauqua Hardware Corp.	150	415
Dahlstrom Manufacturing Co.	150	350
Jamestown Metal Products	90	110
Jamestown Metal Manufacturing Corp.	166	335
Jamestown Plywood Co.	200	155
Watson Industries	68	115
Total	824	1,480

substantial increases in employment under new ownership and management. Since jobs cannot be added to a firm that no longer exists, the total employment of these six firms in mid-1981 should be credited to JALMC.

Dividing the total cost of the program, $931,100, by the 1,480 jobs saved or added yields a cost per job of $629. Compared with other methods of job saving or creating, this is a very reasonable amount. This figure, however, grossly underestimates the benefits of JALMC because it allocates the total 10-year costs according to the benefits derived just from one part of the JALMC program.

As already noted, the LMC plant redesign project at Carborundum saved the company more than $3 million. Since an old and inefficient plant is bound to be shut down sooner or later, this JALMC project has preserved three hundred jobs. Similarly, the AMSCO sink polishing project saved twenty jobs, and the project resulting in a successful bid for $1.5 million in new business a year, forty jobs. The system of the joint union-management team bidding on new jobs at Hopes Windows is estimated to have provided job security for one hundred fifty workers.

While Falconer Glass Industries has not had as deep an involvement in JALMC as other companies mentioned, several periods of LMC activities are thought to have helped improve labor relations and thus to have facilitated company growth from 256 workers in 1974 to 359 in 1981. Recently, facing the need for a major plant expansion and upgrading of its equipment, Falconer management seriously considered a sunbelt state offer of a new plant and a ten-year tax abatement. But when the company was able to negotiate an unusual five-year contract with its union and secure credit for plant modernization and expansion from the Chautauqua County Industrial Development Agency, management decided to remain in Jamestown.

At the time of the 1976 Corry-Jamestown strike, top management was seriously considering trying to sell or shut down the plant. JALMC's involvement with this plant appears to have been important in maintaining about five-hundred jobs.

How has JALMC fared in maintaining employment in manufacturing compared with New York State as a whole or compared with other cities in the state? This is an important question for which there are no definitive statistics to supply an answer. The available figures for the state in the 1970s provide information by counties, and, at this level, do not distinguish between unemployment in manufacturing and that in other lines. There are cities other than Jamestown in Chautauqua County, and some of JALMC's program activities have extended beyond the county or even the state (Corry-Jamestown being in Pennsylvania). Furthermore, JALMC has concentrated its activities primarily in manufacturing.

With these qualifications, let us place Jamestown in the context of the state and in relation to comparable industrial communities. For the two decades from 1953 to 1973, manufacturing jobs declined 23.4 percent in New York (O'Leary 1974), and this decline continued through 1975. For the period from 1975 to 1980, the governor reported a 3 percent increase in manufacturing employment (Carey 1981). The most dramatic improvement in Jamestown occurred earlier, in the first eighteen months of the program. According to the JALMC three-year report (1974), "The unemployment rate had been reduced from 10 percent of the work force in March, 1972, to 4.2 percent in September, 1974."

For city comparisons, Auburn, Watertown, and Utica seem reasonably similar to Jamestown in that they are all upstate cities at considerable distance from major population centers and have important and diversified industrial activities. Auburn and Watertown have roughly the same size labor force as Jamestown; Utica's labor force is about twice as large. A review of average annual unemployment figures for the eight years from 1973 to 1981 shows Jamestown's unemployment is below all three comparison cities for every year throughout that period. The average for the whole period puts Jamestown at 6.80 percent, compared with Watertown at 8.43 percent, Auburn at 9.26 percent, and Utica at 8.82 percent.

To go beyond these rough comparisons would require research beyond the scope of this book, a systematic study of the New York State labor force in recent decades. At the least, these somewhat limited figures support the conclusion that JALMC has had a favorable impact on employment.

JALMC is generally credited with reducing the incidence of labor-management conflict (see table 3). But it is difficult to prove the extent to which JALMC *caused* the sharp drop in strike days lost from the 1960s to the 1970s. There was a substantial reduction in the 1960s, before JALMC came into existence, and undoubtedly the recession of 1974 and the threatened shutdowns reduced labor militancy. Nevertheless, it is widely believed that JALMC had made important contributions to improving the labor climate, and Jamestown received credit in the national media for this achievement. Changing Jamestown's reputation as a bad labor town was important in persuading Cummins Engine Company to take over the abandoned Art Metal Plant and begin the building of a local organization expected to reach fifteen-hundred employees in the 1980s. Furthermore, since strikes at absentee-owned plants lasted almost five times as long as those in locally owned firms, the shift of some of the plants to local control strengthened Jamestown's ability to handle its own problems.

JALMC has extended the methodology of organization development in important respects. Previously, organization development had been limited to a third-party involvement with management. In Jamestown the whole organization, including the union, is involved in the organization development effort. Most well-

TABLE 3. Work Stoppages in Jamestown, 1950–79

	No. Work Stoppages	No. Strike Days
1950–59	63	2,039
1960–69	39	1,442
1970–79	31	749

known productivity and quality of working life projects have been carried out in rich companies that had money and staff to spare. While in some cases major companies, Carborundum, for example, have been involved with JALMC, much of the activity has been carried out in small firms or plants, some of them in precarious financial condition. JALMC could not survive as a luxury to be dispensed with whenever money was short.

JALMC points the way to solution of consultation problems that many small companies face. You may recognize that you need technical assistance, but do you know just what kind of technical assistance is needed, and, if you can afford it, do you know where to find consultants that will do an effective job at reasonable cost? The large and rich firm has great advantages in resolving these problems. It can establish its own internal consulting organization. When a big company needs to bring in outside consultants, its own technical specialists are experienced in dealing with outsiders and can distinguish between those who offer really professional skills and those whose skills are largely confined to selling their wares. The small local firm is at a disadvantage and not only financially. For example, two Jamestown companies in the early stages of JALMC got together to pay $250,000 that they could ill afford to bring in a team of consultants to increase managerial efficiency. While the management people involved saw some immediate gains from this effort, they also suffered serious disruptions in their labor relations and are now inclined to think that they wasted their money.

The lesson to be learned from this case is not one of avoiding out-of-town consultants at all costs. In the Corry-Jamestown case, an outside consultant was used with good results. To the extent that JALMC develops its own professional skills and experience, however, Jamestown firms can acquire local consultants whose previous performance can be readily checked with local labor and management people. If management then decides that outside consultation beyond JALMC is needed, the JALMC staff can work with union and management to help fit the outside consultant into the local scene.

The community-based nature of JALMC offers great advantages in starting and terminating projects. In the usual consultation situation, if management decides to terminate a project, the consultant leaves town and becomes involved in other projects. If, at a later time, union and management people decide that they want to resume work on the lines broken off earlier, they may not be able to bring in consultants with previous experience in their organization. In Jamestown, terminations or failures are not so likely to be permanent. In the cases of AMSCO, Carborundum, and Falconer Glass, some months after projects with JALMC were broken off, management and union leaders agreed to invite JALMC to resume activities.

The benefits of a community-based program extend far beyond the gates of the factories. Jamestown has been building its community organizing capacity. The joint projects carried out within plants and in interorganizational cooperation have been providing valuable experience for social learning. Successes have reinforced the commitment of the participants to this development strategy and have increased their confidence in their own ability and the ability of their fellow citizens to solve the problems of their community. Through JALMC and its related activities, Jamestown has changed in less than a decade from a dying industrial city to an exciting place to live and work.

3.
Lessons from
the Jamestown Experience

Christopher B. Meek, Reed Nelson, and William Foote Whyte

IF THE EXPERIENCES of JALMC are to yield more than a case history of success, we must draw from it lessons that can be applied to other communities. While each community must seek to develop a model appropriate to its own culture and social, political, and economic organization, certain general principles can be derived from the Jamestown case. With this end, we will discuss the charter, staff facilitation process, causes of breakdowns in LMC projects, and finally the relations among the LMC, the labor contract, and the style of managerial leadership.

THE CHARTER

The charter provides the organizational form and rules of the game that serve as a framework for the labor-management process. While the aim of an area LMC is to help build an informal and trusting relationship between the parties, extreme informality can lead to confusion of expectations and failure to find a joint sense of direction. When a local plant considers forming a labor-management committee, a JALMC representative meets separately with the union and management to assess the interest and commitment of both sides and to inform each party of JALMC methods and goals. If both sides respond favorably to the idea, the consultant calls a joint meeting to explore issues to be addressed and to begin developing a charter statement.

The charter sets ground rules for the process of joint problem solving and sets forth the goals, philosophy, and the structure the LMC will assume. Before becoming officially involved, JALMC generally insists that the following elements be incorporated in the charter: (1) Participation will be on a voluntary basis; either party may withdraw at any time. (2) The bargaining rights of the union will be respected. (3) Productivity gains brought about through the LMC will not result in job loss, and gains will be shared between the company and the workers. (4) The LMC will limit itself to noncontractual issues (later we will discuss how this principle may be modified in the course of experience).

A charter setting forth purposes, goals, and general policies offers several benefits to the parties. The quasi-legal structure of a charter is easily understood by union members because of its similarity to the labor contract. Although a charter is not legally binding, it plays an important role in building commitment to the labor-management process. When time and effort have been taken to specify objectives and ground rules in a formal document, those involved are more likely to take the LMC seriously. A charter also provides assurances that those participating will not be penalized for contributing their ideas and viewpoints. Further, the charter can be used for monitoring the committee's progress toward common goals. It enables both parties to steer activities away from subjects that have not been sanctioned for the in-plant LMC. When used in conjunction with yearly strategic planning, the charter can become a powerful tool for providing direction to the program.

The charter provides for a permanent steering committee that creates temporary subcommittees. Rather than promoting worker input only as long as a consultant or facilitator is there to lead the effort, the charter establishes a steering committee to institutionalize worker participation. A major reason for a permanent steering committee is to avoid project fixation. If an LMC is created only to solve one specific problem, there is danger of stagnation when the problem is solved or efforts to solve the problem bog down.

The temporary subcommittees make it possible to bring people with needed resources into the problem-solving process without the restrictions of equal representation or long-term commitment. Although balanced labor-management representation is critical for the policy-making functions of the steering committee, the existence of a strong steering committee permits subcommittees to be more pragmatic in their composition and approach.

The use of subcommittees also allows for involvement by a greater number of people. This is particularly important because of the encapsulation that often occurs in quality of working life projects. Projects become encapsulated when the participants are isolated from other groups in the organization. Lack of widely based participation and support often leads to suspicion and animosity among people who are not involved. Because the LMC process is voluntary and therefore susceptible to pressures within management or labor, the most effective way to avoid encapsulation is to involve a large number of people in the LMC process. The posting of LMC committee minutes, as usually provided for in the charter, is one means of providing information about LMC activities to those who are not participating. While mere posting of minutes is never sufficient to assure good communication, it is a step toward avoiding suspicion about what goes on in labor-management meetings.

After a charter is drawn up, the steering committee, composed of five to eight representatives from each side, chooses one or two problems on which the LMC will work. The steering committee then establishes a subcommittee to work on the problem or problems. The subcommittee may split up further into miniteams to clear up aspects of the project that do not require the attention of a larger group. Having formed its conclusions, the subcommittee formulates recommendations and presents them to the steering committee to be approved, modified, or rejected. Subcommittees are likely to be temporary, ceasing activity when a given project has reached a conclusion.

The steering committee should be a permanent feature of any in-plant LMC program. It is needed to establish priorities for action, to establish subcommittees, to monitor progress of projects, and to work with management in implementing the changes proposed by subcommittees. The steering committee generally meets monthly, and it is desirable for it to meet annually for a one- or two-day conference to review progress, diagnose problems, and take the time needed for long-range planning.

THIRD-PARTY FACILITATION

Those who provided technical assistance for JALMC during its formative years came form one of two backgrounds: they had labor relations experience or an organization development–management consulting background. Over the life of the committee, these two perspectives have fused into a hybrid to combine the best of both approaches. Achieving the combination was not always smooth. Before the present model of labor-management cooperation could emerge, both perspectives had to yield to the realities of the Jamestown setting. A pure labor relations strategy had to be expanded to include concerns about the effectiveness and efficiency of local organizations, and the traditional intervention approach of organization development had to undergo serious modification in order to work in a blue-collar environment with a long history of labor unrest.

The main drawbacks to a strategy based strictly on labor relations are its narrowness of scope and reactivity. The labor relations specialist tends to concentrate on the collective bargaining relationship to the exclusion of other elements in the organizational system. Success then is defined in terms of labor peace without consideration of overall firm performance. While labor peace is an important goal, it neglects many issues that were critical to the success of JALMC in revitalizing local factories.

In a labor relations relationship, demands and complaints are presented to management, which is then expected to take remedial measures. The implicit assumption is that management has the prerogative to run the firm and therefore is responsible for solutions to problems presented by the union. LMC activities that are outgrowths of labor relations programs tend to fall into a pattern of union stimulus–management response, i.e., union complains, management rectifies. At first this stimulus-response approach may stimulate better communication and understanding between labor and management. But eventually management becomes overloaded with union requests, and labor becomes disgruntled as management solutions are long delayed and, when offered, often do not address the problems as perceived by labor. Because management does not gain any direct benefits through hearing union complaints and the union has no involvement in management solutions, the process tends to bog down. The reactive role of the union, always providing criticism of managerial actions without having a role in problem solving eventually erodes trust and good will.

What is needed is active union and worker participation in solving problems. As labor members become directly involved with management in working through the detailed steps of joint problem solving, they take pride in their participation, and management people come to recognize workers as a source of constructive contributions.

Most organization development projects have been implemented with middle management or executive personnel. This has led to intervention techniques with several features incompatible with a union, blue-collar atmosphere. One feature is the use of social science jargon to explain intervention concepts. This tends to legitimize techniques as being scientific, thus increasing their acceptability with well-educated members of the middle class. When such jargon is transferred to the shop floor, it often proves confusing or threatening to people who are not familiar with the linguistic gymnastics of social science. Although this still proves a problem to new consultants, we have found ways to communicate ideas without relying on complicated vocabulary. In earlier experiences with forming in-plant committees, we sought to introduce the concepts in training sessions before asking the participants to focus on concrete problems. Further experience suggested that it would be better to integrate decision-making and problem-solving training into the actual problem-solving process. Rather than teach all steps at first, we now begin by presenting a brief outline of the rules for brainstorming and then actually brainstorming to identify possible issues to be addressed by the LMC. Similarly, the other steps of setting priorities, suggesting and evaluating alternatives, and so forth, are integrated into the actual business of the committee.

With this approach, it is possible to undertake fairly sophisticated projects with a minimum of formal training and within a relatively short time.

Another focus arising from organization development is an emphasis on the present and direct confrontation of problems in group settings. Here again some modifications are needed. In most labor-management situations a cultural barrier created by educational and class disparities separates the two sides. In management circles, actors share a similar level of verbal ability and communication skills. On the labor side, only a few local union officers may have the verbal skills and self-confidence to hold their own with management in discussing the sometimes complex problems that come before the LMC. Furthermore, most workers are accustomed to situations where they must either accept management decisions in silence or aggressively bargain for union rights. Neither of these postures works in a successful LMC. Thus workers are often intimidated by management articulateness or by the meeting setting itself and tend to acquiesce publicly when they have serious reservations that they are unable to articulate during the meeting.

This makes it necessary for the labor-management consultant to play a more involved backstage role than would be expected in a traditional organization development context. Rather than simply collecting worker perceptions and presenting them to management as survey feedback, the labor-management facilitator must develop the ability and confidence of employees to present their views and propose actions responding to their concerns. To do this, the facilitator must spend time with union members helping them to contemplate their reactions to LMC meetings and to formulate strategies and proposals that reflect their feelings and interests. This contrasts with an approach in which a group simply confronts issues as they arise in team-building sessions or sensitivity training.

Similarly, the consultant may have to spend time developing managers' sensitivity to differences between labor-management meetings and regular management meetings. Managers are often used to giving orders to workers without discussing the merits of those orders or considering alternative means of attaining an objective. Even traditional contract language serves to heighten the characterization of the union as a passive or reactive entity. Convincing management people in general and particularly CEOs of small firms that worker input must be seriously considered and patiently cultivated can sometimes be a mammoth task. Since managers customarily take the initiative in dealing with labor, the facilitator's efforts to reorient management to the LMC process may be even more important than the consulting on the labor side.

Another reason for not concentrating so much on the present is the importance of the past in labor-management relations, especially in Jamestown. Most LMCs arise in response to turbulent labor relations. It takes much positive shared experience before people can feel safe disclosing their true feelings. Before long-standing mistrust between union and management is overcome, facilitators may have to meet several times with the parties separately to allay fears and to provide a chance for each side to talk freely and raise issues too sensitive to approach directly. Often the parties have met only at the bargaining table, and it takes considerable coaching before those involved become comfortable with the difference between the bargaining relationship and an LMC relationship.

Finally, the Jamestown emphasis on avoiding dependence and enabling LMC members to run their own committees requires less consultant involvement in meetings but increases involvement behind the scenes. A self-managing LMC is an explicit goal of JALMC, so care is taken to encourage in-plant committees to chair their own meetings. Under the Jamestown model, the consultant will not necessarily assume the direction of a meeting that is being run poorly, or intervene to analyze group dynamics as would likely happen in a traditional organization development effort. He or she will be more likely to contact people before or after meetings to plan, solicit comments, and make suggestions.

Because the consultant takes a backseat role in meetings, the skill of LMC leaders in managing their own group processes becomes critical. Although the general principles of labor-managment relationships apply to all actors in the LMC process, the leadership role has special ramifications that merit additional consideration. Labor-managment committees are fundamentally participative devices, but this does not eliminate the need for effective coordination and guidance. Nothing enlivens a labor-management committee like the belief that it is moving toward some mutually valued goal, and nothing will dampen spirits like the suspicion of lack of direction and movement. We have noted in Jamestown and in other settings that effective leadership is necessary for group progress (Whyte 1950). Ability to keep a group moving toward its objectives without dominating or alienating members seems to be in short supply, both among managers and union personnel. Thus it is very important for the facilitator to develop leaders' process skills.

The key to managing the LMC group process, and other task-oriented groups, is finding the optimum balance between providing direction and fostering group input. The ideal mixture of direction and participation varies from situation to situation. Particularly when an LMC is new, more freedom may be needed to explore the new relationship between labor and management. But an LMC cannot function indefinitely as an unstructured rap session, as experience during the labor relations phase of JALMC bears out. The chairperson must learn to sense when all parties have had their say and the group is ready to move on or, when no one is saying anything, discussion needs to be stimulated.

This is an area that can require considerable time and expertise, and the consultant may occasionally want to provide formal training outside regular meetings. Some fairly basic instructions, however, can often improve chairperson performance in a short time. A short primer on how to hold a meeting has been one of JALMC's most successful training aids: just the ability to prepare an agenda and hold to it can be very valuable. One group improved meetings considerably by agreeing on a time limit for agenda items and actually monitoring progress with an egg timer. This technique is not for all groups nor for every meeting of every group. This same LMC has also postponed agenda items for a later meeting when it has become apparent that some important issue has escaped the attention of the committee. Such simple devices should not be disregarded as too elementary for experienced managers and union leaders.

A major role of the consultant is that of providing information or perspectives that the client organization does not have. The emphasis on developing self-sufficiency in LMCs does not mean isolation from outside ideas, and there is no reason for a facilitator to remain passive when he or she has information relevant to the business at hand. The varied experience of LMCs in the Jamestown area and elsewhere provides a fund of information that can be helpful to the LMC efforts of individual organizations. The facilitator can sometimes accelerate progress by feeding in ideas gained elsewhere.

Prospects for such intervention are best when the committee has arrived on its own at some specific problem about which the facilitator has special experience or knowledge. Not only does this improve chances that the facilitator's idea will be considered carefully, it also reduces the danger that a project irrelevant to the concerns of the organization will be undertaken because it is a favorite approach of the third party. The facilitator's knowledge of social inventions generated elsewhere becomes a most valuable resource for the committee. Ideally, facilitator involvement should wane over time, but no LMC reaches the point at which perspectives from the outside are of no value. As in the case of complex process skills, it may be useful for the consultant to present more complicated concepts or projects in separate training sessions that do not impinge on the actual business of the committee. Here, the facilitator may assume a more central role in organizing and presenting information for consideration by committee members.

BUILDING A LEARNING COMMUNITY

When the role is played in traditional fashion, the consultant may make the organization increasingly dependent upon outside assistance. This potential problem was noted early by JALMC staff and members, with the result that the abilities of Jamestown people to learn from each other are now increasing. JALMC staff members stimulated the first intercompany exchanges of information and ideas. The pattern seems so well established now that when union and management people in one company recognize they are facing a problem dealt with successfully by an LMC in another company, they take the initiative to tap the experience of labor and management in that company. This pattern of interplant exchanges is reinforced by periodic seminars and by the annual two-day conference in which labor and management people from the various plants report their experiences with LMCs and discuss problems and achievements with fellow Jamestowners and outsiders. Aside from its ceremonial function of strengthening labor-management solidarity, the annual steak fry provides an occasion for facilitating communication among companies and local unions.

Since not all in-plant LMCs have carried out successful projects, Jamestown provides an opportunity to learn from failures as well as successes. The most common failures are those committees that die through neglect. In several Jamestown firms, LMCs were introduced with much fanfare but gradually atrophied because of lack of management commitment.

Some CEOs get involved with in-plant LMCs because LMCs are fashionable, but they do not have any real interest in worker input. This seems particularly the case with owners of small to medium size factories who are used to keeping close control over every aspect of their operation. Because the CEO keeps close tabs on the whole operation, he is pressed for time and often misses LMC meetings. If a meeting is held in the CEO's absence, its results will be inconclusive because he was not involved in their formulation. As one union man described it, "X runs a one-man shop. He got into labor-management because all his friends did, but he never went to meetings. And if he isn't there, it doesn't matter whether you have a meeting or not." Given this scenario, meetings become rarer and rarer until they cease outright.

In other cases, management may withdraw if the plant's chief executive finds the program threatening to his style of leadership. For example, in one case Keidel was shocked to find that, after several highly successful projects, the executive had decided to discontinue working with "outsiders." He explained that his idea of quality of working life involved bowling leagues, picnics, and "that kind of stuff." He told Keidel that he was afraid that the in-plant LMC was "stirring up the people," and that on second thought he had decided that he liked having the company's twenty-odd departments operating like "islands."

Breakdowns can also result from union reluctance or mistrust. Usually LMCs do not even get past the planning stages when the union is especially distrustful of management intentions. Occasionally, however, such a union will consent to become involved in an LMC for the purpose of proving that management cannot be trusted. Union members will wait until management does something that can be exploited as an issue. Then the union will resign from the committee in angry protest. This problem is most likely to occur when the union is experiencing an internal power struggle. One group will use involvement in labor-management as a lever to oust present leaders, whom they claim have sold out to management. These breakdowns are usually stormy affairs and leave bad feeling within the union as well as between the union and management.

Once a committee gets past the barriers of management autocracy and union reluctance, the next step is to find some problem for labor and management to work on jointly. If management is facing an urgent problem, it is easy to decide on the first project, but this sort of beginning for an LMC may lead to "projectitis." The members, and particularly managers, look upon the LMC as a means of solving a particular problem. When that problem is solved, the parties see no need to continue meetings. In other words, if an LMC is visualized in terms of projects rather than as a problem-solving process, then breakdowns are inevitable.

Another source of breakdowns is encapsulation, a phenomenon that has been observed elsewhere (Trist, Susman, and Brown 1977; Strauss 1955). The project is successful in that management and the workers directly involved have benefited, but it was limited to workers in a particular department and precipitated opposition from a larger number of workers who received no benefits and possibly saw their own interests threatened. Encapsulation is likely to be a particularly serious problem in cases where the union local is sharply divided into competing factions.

The breakdown at AMSCO illustrates the encapsulation problem, as well as having other interesting complications. The issues leading to local union withdrawal from the plant LMC arose out of the self-managing work team activities in the polishing department. The department had been an unpopular place to work so that, in general, workers with sufficient seniority sought to move to higher paying and higher status departments. Consequently, with two exceptions, those in the polishing department were young, low-seniority workers with low status in the social system of the factory.

The beginnings of the polishers' problems with workers in other departments can be traced to the decision to pay a ten dollar weekly bonus to all members of the self-managing team. The plant manager at first balked at the idea of such a bonus, fearing that it would cause "jealousy" and "political trouble." Eldred argued that such bonuses were customarily paid workers joining self-managing teams in recognition of their increased value to the company because now they were expected to master all jobs in their department and even take over responsibilities carried by supervisors in traditionally managed departments.

Although the bonus was a small percentage of the paychecks, it had a marked symbolic effect. One polisher later explained, "The bonus was pretty much like a sliver that started as just a little pain but gradually worked its way in with other irritations and then finally festered into a big sore."

The success of the polishers in productivity and quality of workmanship built up the self-confidence and enthusiasm among them that markedly altered their roles both inside and outside the plant. JALMC staffers were interested in being able to demonstrate successful cases to other management and union people, professors, students, and reporters in Jamestown and elsewhere. This led to invitations to representatives of the polishers to tell their story in local conferences and occasionally in meetings in other cities. The polishers enjoyed the local limelight and the all-expenses-paid trips to perform before audiences, including prominent members of the quality of working life movement.

Within the plant, whenever a new LMC project was announced, polishers volunteered to work on it. Their success with their own project made them well qualified for further work organized in a similar manner, including tasks of plantwide significance, such as the product costing project. So regularly were they chosen by the plant LMC for new projects that the whole labor-management cooperation program at AMSCO tended to be identified with the polishers.

Although the polishers were efficient on their jobs, they had problems disciplining themselves. On one occasion several members of the team started engaging in horseplay, shooting water at each other. This incident grew to involve nearly the whole team, and two employees went so far as to shoot a fire extinguisher. Eventually, the horseplay stopped, but by that time nearly everyone in the plant knew what had happened. Under other circumstances the employees involved would have been issued a warning slip and possibly suspended because of the safety hazard they had created. In this case there was no supervisor. The department as a whole was supervision, and they obviously did not discipline themselves. The incident and several others like it deeply angered senior union members as well as the majority of first-line supervisors who saw their jobs threatened by the team concept.

Plant manager Laughner was aware of the discipline problem, but he hesitated to intervene because he valued the enthusiasm and creativity of this work group and did not want to take actions that might appear to run counter to the maintenance and growth of a participatory system.

> What we did is turn a bunch of young guys loose on a few older employees, and we started to generate so much interest and energy out of the younger people that they completely disregarded the needs of the older people. And they completely took over the department without any formal announcement that they had the authority to do this or even the ability to do it, in some people's minds.
>
> I wound up with a terrible safety problem. They were down there feeling they could do anything they wanted to. They were riding wheels around and hanging dirty pictures on the wall and all kinds of nutsy things that young people will do. You can expect it—I just never anticipated it.
>
> So we had a situation where a lot of people felt that the self-managing department was acting pretty peculiarly, and they were saying, "What the hell does the company put up with that bunch of screwballs down there for?" We weren't blind. We knew what was going on there too, but we thought that it was a natural progression in these kinds of things. Okay, we didn't like what was going on down there totally, but we thought it was kind of natural.

Eldred gave a similar interpretation of the problems:

> The members of the self-managing team really developed a lot of enthusiasm for their work and were seriously concerned about the polishing department's productiviy. Unfortunately, their enthusiasm sometimes led to some pretty obnoxious behavior. You see, when the team would get

ahead in their work they would sometimes leave their work stations and go and badger the people in the other departments that fed them work. They weren't very diplomatic and would say things like, "What's the matter with you guys? You're holding us up!"

You can imagine the kind of trouble that created. I told them to cut it out, but I don't think they really took me seriously.

Eldred had anticipated the encapsulation problem, and, only a month after the polishers' project was started, he had proposed that two other self-managing teams be established in other higher status departments. Opposition by the union stewards blocked this proposal.

The polishers' project had been established for a six-month trial. The polishers were able to get the local union to support two three-month extensions, but by the time they came back to urge the third extension, many of the older and more powerful union members had become particularly hostile to the group. After a bitter and heated argument, the polishers were overwhelmingly defeated in a vote in the union meeting. One polisher described this union meeting:

> I will say there was a lot of jealousy. It got so bad that we had a union meeting on Monday night, and the radicals who were against the project got a group together to make sure it didn't go on. They said something like, "The labor-management pilot project is over. The time limit for this pilot project has expired. You were only supposed to get six months and then you got three more and after that expired you got another three months extension. It's been a whole year and you guys are still going with this dumb project. It's over, and we want it stopped! As of tomorrow morning there's not going to be any more pilot projects. You guys are supposed to have a boss, and there will be a boss!"
>
> They really hated the idea of us telling ourselves what do to instead of having a foreman. It was so stupid and immature. You couldn't pound it into their heads with a twenty-pound sledge hammer. They told us, "Tomorrow morning you guys will go down there and stand around until the foreman comes and tells you what to do!"

Within two months after the scrapping of the polishers' self-managing team, the whole labor-management cooperative program came to an abrupt end. According to the plant manager, the end came when he was proposing a major expansion of the program in order to avoid layoffs. Laughner took the new program to the plant LMC.

I approached them in this fashion: "Gentlemen, we are going to have a layoff, and it's going to be pretty severe." I think thirty-some people were going to be laid off, which in this place is pretty severe. I told the union, "We are willing to retain some of these people if you are willing to sit with me and develop a series of things which I perceive need to be done, and which I believe you perceive need to be done, and we'll siphon some of these people off on to what I prefer to call project work."

They seemed to think that was a pretty good idea. As union representatives, they felt that it was their job to help keep jobs here and stablize employment in this particular case. And so we sat down as a committee and made a list of what turned out to be thirty-seven items that we felt needed to be done. Some of which were mine, some of which were their's, some were involved, and some were very superficial. What I wanted to do was get a lot of different people involved from outside of that department (you know, the self-managing team) so that a lot of people could experience all of this. We wanted to do a welding program. We wanted to do a relayout of the assembly area. There were lots of things that would have got lots of people involved.

So we finally boiled it down to where I felt I had an obligation to retain people who had four or more years seniority. I think that came down to twelve. That's a lot of money on a yearly basis. We also had to agree on who was going to work and not going to work as coordinators for these projects, and we got into a hassle over this.

What we had was thirty-seven projects and twelve people from the factory to work on them with some guidance from the rest of the factory. So there were more projects than people to go around. So we tried to prioritize them and say that the twelve people would be absorbed in these three projects for the next three months, and after that we may pick twelve more and do it like that. But when the union went back to make their presentation to the membership, they got into an argument over who would do this work. The most senior man in some cases would say, "Hey, I want to go into the office and do that, and I have the most seniority so I should be permitted to do that." And in other cases a senior man would say, "Hey, I want to stay out here and run my machine. It should be the least senior man that should do that." So here I was, Jim Laughner saying, "If we've got a five-man team working on welding, I've got to have at least one experienced welder on it or I'm going to have to teach the whole group to weld before we even start." So the intermingling of these philosophies caused the union to ask for a special union meeting. The union president came into my office and asked for the meeting at 2:00 p.m. They had the largest turnout for a union meeting they had ever had, even for the ratification of a contract. In fact, everybody was there.

Just before the meeting the union president came in and talked with me and told me what he was going to do. I didn't want to be giving this fellow advice, but when I heard what he planned, it really scared me. He and his committee had fallen into a great deal of disfavor because they were totally dedicated to this concept of cooperation. Just a month before this big vote we'd put him, his committee, and some members of the self-managing team on an airplane and flew them to Philadelphia where they did a dog and pony show. And they had also flown to Washington, D.C., to talk at a conference at the National Quality of Working Life Center, and they had been totally stunned by this. Anyway, a lot of union folks were pretty jealous about these trips, and so I was pretty worried when the union president came in and told me, "I'm going to put this proposal before the whole body and if they don't accept it, I am going to resign." That in fact was just what he did. He got up in the union meeting and basically said these words, "I have a proposal to put in front of you and if you don't agree with me, then you're voting down labor-management altogether and I'm going to resign!" And what with him being in such disfavor anyway, everybody clapped and then they voted everything out the door in one big sweep—him, the idea of employment maintenance, and the whole labor-management program.

Thus ended one of the most far-reaching programs in labor-management cooperation in Jamestown. Furthermore, the effects of the breakdown extended beyond the AMSCO plant. Since the breakdown was widely interpreted as being caused by the problems with the polishing department self-managing team, after it, other union and management leaders tended to shy away from any innovations involving autonomous work groups or self-managing teams.

The breakdown at Carborundum is of special interest because it occurred shortly after the completion of what is perhaps the most spectacularly successful in-plant project of the JALMC. Management maintains that it was common knowledge that the redesign project would have to be paid for through increased productivity and a corresponding reduction in employment. Union leaders state that they never agreed to any job loss associated with the plant redesign, and it is clear that the extent of the job loss was never discussed or negotiated in the implementation of the LMC project.

When the redesigned plant commenced operations, management laid off thirty-two workers, approximately 10 percent of the work force. Management claims that only six of the thirty-two were accounted for by the modernization project and that the other twenty-six were being laid off in response to a downturn in business. Since all the layoffs occurred with the completion of the project, however, workers naturally attributed the total job loss to that project. In the face of widespread worker protests, the union president felt he had no alternative other than to pull the union out of the LMC.

As an epilogue, it should be added that, even without a joint steering committee, union and management continued cooperation on one joint project involving the orientation of new employees. As time passed and all but six of those laid off were rehired, union and management leaders have again got together to make a new start with a labor-management committee.

Could breakdowns such as occurred at AMSCO and Carborundum have been avoided?

The Carborundum case indicates the necessary linkage between the LMC program and job security. The plant manager argues persuasively that the redesign and rebuilding of the plant were essential to job security in the long run, but, like other people, workers have to live in the short run also. The project caused a short-run drop in the number of workers needed. Without layoffs, the reduction in the work force could have been achieved over a period of time through retirements and voluntary resignations. Perhaps the breakdown could have been avoided if the manager and the LMC had worked out a plan to utilize the workers not needed in production on special projects, as Laughner hoped to do at AMSCO.

Important as job security is for labor-management cooperation, the AMSCO case indicates that this is not the only problem confronting the parties. In fact, it is ironic to note that it was Laughner's effort to maintain job security with special projects that precipitated the termination of the whole cooperative program. Since self-managing work groups have been used successfully in many plants in many countries, we cannot assume that the concept itself was unsound. Therefore, we must examine the process of implementation. The growing resistance to the polishers' project appears to have arisen out of a disturbance to the established status system of the plant. A group of young, inexperienced, low-seniority, and therefore low status workers were given freedom from supervision and special treatment. They gained unaccustomed prominence in the plant and in the outside world—plus a financial bonus. Suppose the self-managing team idea had been introduced first in a department of older and higher seniority workers, enjoying above-average pay and having influence in the local union. Adding to the prominence of people already prominent in the plant might have been less disturbing to the social system. If that strategy had been followed, it might have been easier to spread the self-managing teams to other departments.

Of course, such a program requires the manager and the LMC to recognize that the introduction and maintenance of self-managing teams not only involves changes in the relations among workers directly involved but also requires far-reaching changes in organization structure, the number of supervisors required, the style of managerial leadership, interdepartmental relations, job descriptions and classifications, and, therefore, the collective bargaining relationship. If the self-managing work team is simply introduced into the first department where it seems to meet some immediate needs, there is a high probability that the project will run into adverse reactions from other parts of the social system.

The AMSCO case also illustrates the need to link freedom with responsibility. The polishers responded superbly to the challenge of getting their work done but were unable to discipline themselves or to manage their relations with other work groups. Furthermore, while a self-managing team should require far less supervisory guidance and policing than the conventional work group, there will always be a need for someone in management to help the workers develop their team, manage their relations with other work units, and discipline themselves and to observe their progress and problems so as to be able to intervene before small problems become large crises.

Even when breakdowns are followed months later by new beginnings, those breakdowns suggest to us that the labor-management cooperative process is likely to be ejected from the plant as it runs afoul of established patterns of managerial leadership and labor relations. If we visualize the factory as a social system made up of mutually dependent parts into which a new part, the LMC, is introduced, we see that it is impossible to introduce this one change while holding everything else constant. The new element will have an effect on other parts of the social system, and those other parts will react to the new element. Therefore, labor and management cannot afford to limit planning to the ways of introducing the LMC. They need also to reflect upon the effect of the LMC on the total social system and the effects of the surrounding parts of the social system on the LMC.

THE LMC, COLLECTIVE BARGAINING, AND MANAGERIAL PREROGATIVES

It is an article of faith among many consultants that the labor-management process must be kept separate from collective bargaining. Implicit in this axiom is the assumption that the LMC is also to be kept separate from managerial prerogatives, since these are generally spelled out in labor contracts.

We are now inclined to argue that this principle is a convenient fiction during the peiod of starting a labor-management committee but not to be taken seriously as the parties advance beyond the beginning stages. In the beginning this principle gives the parties a sense of security. Suppose the consultant approached the parties with what we now consider a realistic interpretation, "If you want this new labor-management process to make its potentially great contribution to workers and to management, you are going to have to make major changes in the style of managerial leadership, abandon some cherished managerial prerogatives, and ignore or renegotiate certain parts of the labor contract." Such an introduction would abort most projects before they get started.

Nevertheless, we suspect that the realistic interpretation is increasingly accepted as at least being implicit by leaders of labor and management in companies that have been most successful in developing the cooperative problem-solving process. Sometimes, if closely questioned and aware that they will not be quoted in print, they will accept the interpretation. For example, in a recent conference, Whyte asked the vice president for industrial relations of a company known for success with the labor-management process how that process affected managerial prerogatives. He replied, "Management prerogatives are out the window. We just work together to solve our problems."

At the same conference, Whyte posed the following problem to union leaders: The parties have agreed to increase productivity and are working together toward this objective. In Department X a machine breaks down. The machine is manned by an experienced worker. He has observed a maintenance man repair the machine often enough so he believes he can do the repair himself in just a few minutes time. Or the foreman, having had similar work experience, could easily make the same repair himself. The alternative is to call a maintenance man and lose an hour of production waiting until someone is free to do the repair. The contract states that only workers attached to the maintenance department are allowed to repair machines. What does a worker or foreman do in such a case, ignore the contract and make the repair or step aside and call for the maintenance man? The union leaders had no difficulty with that question. They replied, in effect, ignore the contract.

If interpreted literally, many labor contracts are straitjackets that prevent the parties from taking actions that otherwise could seem fair and reasonable. The rigidities of the contract do not arise accidentally. They are the natural outgrowths of years of struggle in which neither party trusted the other and so both parties bargained to achieve clauses that would protect their rights and limit the freedom of the other party. As the parties begin the cooperative process and achieve some initial successes, they come to trust each other and have less need of contractual protection. The contract no longer dictates behavior, yet it continues to exist as a fallback mechanism to which either party can resort if cooperation breaks down.

This is not to suggest that ignoring the contract is a general principle to be applied to all problems. Consider, for example, a problem that recently came up in the Rath Packing Company. Because of a decline in one line of business, a plant superintendent was thinking of laying off thirteen workers in one department. He pointed out that, according to the very detailed seniority clauses that had been negotiated in the 1950s when the company was expanding, the layoff of thirteen workers could precipitate a bumping process resulting in ninety job moves. Workers would be moving throughout the plant from department to department and from shift to shift, breaking up work teams, placing workers in jobs with which they were unfamiliar, reducing operating efficiency, and creating morale problems.

This illustrates the kind of systemic problem that cannot be resolved simply by ignoring the contract. The thirteen workers to be dropped from one department will obviously insist upon their bumping rights wherever they have the necessary seniority. This is also not a problem that can be resolved in a traditional adversarial confrontation. Management agreed long ago in this case that, when workers can perform the jobs in question, seniority shall determine job placement. Unfortunately, that principle does not specify what kind of a seniority system will best meet the now jointly recognized needs for efficient production and job security. The parties need to develop a joint study process in which they eventually devise a new system to be then ratified in a revised labor contract.

If the labor-management process is to go beyond cosmetic changes, then any LMC project is likely to impinge on contractual clauses covering job descriptions, job classifications, work loads, and workplace staffing. Therefore, the parties must be willing and able to explore the necessary interrelations between the labor-management process and collective bargaining. This does not mean that the parties should agree at the outset to abandon managerial prerogatives and to disregard the contract when convenient.

This would be asking them to forget all their past experience with each other. It does mean that the parties should proceed with an exploratory frame of mind, following labor-management problems where they lead, dealing with contractual issues as they stand in the way of solving practical problems, and recognizing that they are building a new social system that will be more effective in serving human and economic needs than their former ways of working together or against each other.

4.
Can You
Buy Your Job?

Tove Helland Hammer, Robert N. Stern, and
William Foote Whyte

WHAT CAN WORKERS, community leaders, union leaders, and members of local management do to save jobs when corporate headquarters announces an impending shutdown? Until about 1970, there seemed nothing to do other than urge the top management to reverse its decision and, when such appeals failed, as they always did, to urge management to make some financial provisions to help laid-off workers relocate and find new jobs. In the 1970s, this fatalistic dependence on the will of top management began to give way to locally organized campaigns to save the jobs through buying the plant.

Since early 1976 we have been studying cases in which jobs have been saved through conversion to employee or employee-community ownership. We have also been interested in the relationship between employee ownership and worker participation in management. We wanted to know whether increased worker participation followed upon the ownership shift and, if so, in what forms and with what consequences. If no changes from the previous styles of management and labor relations occurred, what were the possible consequences of this absence of change?

Members of our research group have carried out intensive case studies of Byers Transport Limited, a large trucking firm in western Canada, Vermont Asbestos Group in Lowell, Vermont, Saratoga Knitting Mill in Saratoga Springs, New York, Mohawk Valley Community Corporation in Herkimer, New York, and Rath Packing Company in Waterloo, Iowa. In addition, we have gathered, directly and indirectly, data of a less comprehensive nature from a large number of other employee-owned firms. The purpose of this chapter is to interpret for labor, management, and community leaders what we have learned regarding the problems and potentials of saving jobs through employee or employee-community ownership.

THREE MYTHS ABOUT SHUTDOWNS

It is important to dispel three myths supporting the fatalistic view that if a big company decides to shut down a plant, there is nothing local people can do to save the jobs in that plant. The first myth is the belief that a big company would not shut down a plant that was making profits and that therefore any plant to be abandoned cannot be expected to become viable for another owner. Especially with conglomerates, there have been cases in which the plant slated to be shut down has been a steady money-maker, but has not been yielding the level of profits desired by top management. In such a case, top management may use the economic rationale that the company's capital would be better employed in more profitable lines of activity. Because of this logic, many profitable plants have been abandoned.

In other cases, the unprofitability of the plant may be traced to a management practice of neglecting maintenance and modernization investments in order to shift its capital to other corporate units (Bluestone and Harrison 1982). If substantial funds for modernization can be raised, in some cases the plant can become economically viable again.

The second myth is that if a plant promised to be profitable, private investors would come forward and buy it. The fact that private investors have not come forward is then taken as proof that the plant must inevitably be a losing proposition and can only be kept alive through government subsidies.

But consider the case of Bates Manufacturing Company in Lewiston, Maine. When local management got together with the workers on an employee stock ownership plan, which was supported by an $8 million loan at 10.25 percent guaranteed to 90 percent by the Farmers Home Administration, management calculated that the new company would be able to pay off the loan, make substantial investments in modernizing plant and equipment, and still earn a profit of 7 percent on invested capital. Consider the situation of private investors, having no interest in Lewiston and seeking only a good and safe return on their money. Would they come forward to invest in a company in the depressed and highly competitive textile industry, with the expectation of making no more than a 7 percent return?

For the 1,100 workers whose jobs were saved at Bates, the financial considerations were quite different. They were not thinking of 7 percent or 3 percent or 0 percent on their money but of jobs promising them $8,000 or more a year for as long as the company survived. Furthermore, since the employee stock ownership plan involved purchasing stock for the workers out of pretax profits of the company, workers did not even have to lay out their own cash to buy their jobs. The owners of small businesses and taxpayers of Lewiston were also vitally concerned about the future of a major source of employment in their city.

A third myth is that big business management is so efficient that employees and local managers could hardly hope to do better than a big company that is abandoning a plant. In other words, in cases where the local plant has indeed been losing money, an employee-owned firm is bound to fail.

While we do not wish to make any generalizations about the level of efficiency of management of big companies, we have documented enough cases where losses of the local plant can be traced directly to gross mismanagement from corporate headquarters to suggest that the fact that the local plant is losing money does not necessarily mean that it is doomed to failure under any form of ownership.

In recent decades, many management strategists have come to

the conclusion that they can make more money by buying a company than by building their own company. Since antitrust legislation stands in the way of mergers of firms in the same line of business, the recent merger trend has been toward the building of conglomerates. Here, the management strategists have misapplied a sound principle for investing in the stock market by private individuals or organizations: minimize risks by building up a portfolio of investments in diverse fields. The conglomerate strategist assumes that it will be to the advantage of his company to own a diverse range of subsidiaries so that when one subsidiary drops in profitability another will gain, and the overall company performance will be strong and steady.

The problem with this reasoning is that, whereas the individual private investor has no influence on decisions of the companies in which he or she owns stock, the top executive taking over other companies is buying the power to make the basic management decisions. The very fact that the conglomerate is taking over a company in a different line of business from any of its other subsidiaries is likely to mean that members of conglomerate top management have no experience or expertise in this newly acquired enterprise. This unfamiliarity increases the likelihood that top management will make decisions that have severe, negative effects on the performance of such subsidiaries (to be sure, these consequences can be avoided if top management allows its new subsidiary to operate with substantial autonomy).

The refutation of these myths should not lead to the assumption that it is easy or even always possible to save jobs through employee ownership. On the contrary, there are enormous problems to be resolved before the employee-owned firm emerges from a plant shutdown. Nevertheless, it is sometimes possible to save jobs through such an ownership shift. Even if it should prove possible to save only one plant out of three or one plant out of five, there is still an enormous potential for saving hundreds of thousands of jobs over a period of years.

ANTICIPATING THE SHUTDOWN CRISIS

Chapter 2 examined the problems and potentials of saving jobs in a privately owned firm through programs of labor-management cooperation. Obviously, it is more in the interest of workers to participate in a joint program with management to save jobs under existing ownership than to take the chance that, when the plant shuts down, they will be able to buy it and save their jobs. While prevention is to be preferred to cure, management may have decided to shut down the plant and be unwilling to consider any measures that might keep it in operation under the existing ownership. When the plant actually shuts down, its customers go elsewhere, and the skilled workers who would be essential to reopening the plant have the best opportunity to find employment elsewhere and are likely to be lost to the potential work force. Therefore, those leading the negotiations are in a better position to make a success of the employee-owned plant if they have some months lead time before the shutdown so that there is a chance of retaining the key people and the market for the plant's products.

While workers and community people have an obvious interest in wanting the earliest possible notification of an impending plant shutdown, management people are likely to have economic reasons for delaying such an announcement until shortly before the event. Management may be concerned that early announcement of a closing date will lead customers to shift their orders elsewhere to assure themselves of a continuing supply. Management may also be concerned that early announcement will lead skilled workers to look for other jobs and that the company will lose some key people for keeping the plant operating for the remaining months or weeks.

What can workers and community people do to anticipate a shutdown if management delays the announcement? It should be recognized that shutting down a plant is no simple matter, so we can assume that planning activities have been going on for some months before the shutdown date (Kelly and Webb 1979). Furthermore, it is unlikely that local management officials ever are completely surprised regarding a shutdown decision. Generally, such a decision has been under discussion for some time in top management, so that local management people have been aware at least of the possibility of a shutdown. As local management officials meet with other management people and city government people socially or for other purposes, the possibility of a shutdown is almost certain to come up in casual conversation. Rumors about potential plant closings may circulate in the community for many months before the actual event. Such rumors, however, may not be very helpful to employees and community people because they fix no time for the event, and furthermore they may foretell an event that never does take place.

Union leaders, in bargaining with local management, may encounter the argument that, if the union secures the gains it seeks, management will be forced to close the plant. Again, however, this signal may not be very helpful because union negotiators may have had previous experience with such shutdown threats when the plant continued operating even after a settlement close to the union's initial demands. They may thus be inclined to dismiss the threat as simply a bargaining tactic. Perhaps they may probe the seriousness of the threat by calling upon management to open its books for union examination. This tactic is unlikely to be very useful because many managements follow a policy of not disclosing their plant financial figures, so the refusal to provide the figures cannot necessarily be taken as an indication that management spokesmen are exaggerating the plight of the plant.

Beyond leakage of information from local management officials to employees and community people, there are concrete signs of an impending plant closing. The company may reduce the number of people employed in local management until only a skeleton staff remains. This may well mean that the plant becomes able only to produce routine items and is no longer able to fill more complex orders—and of course, the falling off of such orders is a further sign of the aproaching end.

Management may also change its approach to contract negotiations. Say that in the past it has been customary for management to call upon the union to have a planning meeting a month or two months before the expiration of the contract. Now management allows such dates to pass without any action, thus unintentionally providing a signal that the company is considering shutting down the plant.

While it may be impossible to take any concrete steps until management makes an official announcement of a date for the plant shutdown, it can still be extremely important for those who may eventually want to consider buying the plant to begin discussing among themselves what information they need and what financial and political contacts they need to develop if they are to be in a position to move quickly and effectively in organizing themselves and community supporters to meet the shutdown crisis.

The success of a campaign to save jobs through employee ownership requires some degree of cooperation from the corporation owning the plant. In the 1970s managements at first failed to take seriously the possibility of selling to an employee or employee-community organization and were reluctant to cooperate with such a plan. In the 1980s we see a growing number of cases in which corporate management took the initiative in suggesting employee ownership as an alternative to a shutdown.

Although one might think it would always be in the interest of the owning corporation to sell the plant rather than simply to close it down and leave it idle, in fact, several factors have weighed against cooperation with local people. In one case, the machinery in the plant was not only modern and in good condition but was of a highly efficient type not readily available in this country. Management estimated that the company would make more money selling the equipment and writing off the buildings, thus gaining substantial tax advantages, than what it could expect to receive from local purchasers. In this case, management changed the shutdown decision only under pressure of a U.S. senator, who reminded the chief executive officer that the senator's office had been frequently called upon by company officials to help on their business problems. If they declined to negotiate reasonably with the local people, he announced that in the future the doors of his offices would be closed to the company.

Management's stance may be influenced by the possibility of competition from its former plant. That is, if the plant being sold would compete with other plants of the company, then management has a material interest weighing against such a sale.

Since a plan to buy the plant must be supported by a feasibility study, the financial figures and operating costs for the plant are of great importance to any potential buyers. Therefore, those interested in helping the employees buy the plant will ask local management to make those figures available. Such a request is often refused on the grounds that the figures represent proprietary information that could be used against the company by competitors and unions representing workers in other plants. If management refuses to make such figures available, this imposes a serious barrier upon the organizing group. In one case, those interested in helping the employees buy the plant had to raise $110,000 in order to contract with an engineering consulting firm for a feasibility study and then had to exercise pressure through several channels to pursuade management to let the consultants into the plant so they could see the equipment and get some idea of its condition. Even so, the consultants were forced to rely upon estimates whose validity could have been improved by direct access to company experience.

By way of contrast, in another case, the necessary figures were secured and put together within forty-eight hours without any expense for outside consultants, although here project organizers received substantial help from an economic development administration university technical assistance center. Key members of local management were planning to stay with the plant if it became employee-owned, so they could provide facts and figures from their own files at no cost.

In the early stages of our studies, we encountered company reluctance to deal with representatives of the employees, apparently because of a patronizing attitude on the part of top company officials. They could not believe that, if they in their wisdom had decided to shut down the plant, employees and local people could have any chance of success with that facility. In some of these cases, leaders of the employee organization believed that management resistance was motivated by the fear of embarrassment if it turned out that the plant abandoned by the company later proved to be highly successful. Since no spokesperson will acknowledge that a company is declining to sell the plant to the employees because it fears they will be too successful with it, there is no way of documenting this motive.

Conditions that may make the owning corporation more receptive to employee ownership may be inferred from factors having the opposite effect. If the plant to be sold to employees will not be making products that compete with any lines of the company's remaining operations, conglomerate decision makers then can anticipate no future damage to their market position through such a transaction. Decision makers may also be inclined to sell to employees job shops where the amount of capital involved relative to labor is small. With such a labor-intensive operation, the owning corporation has little to gain through a tax write-off and so may be more willing to negotiate a sale to employees.

There are also political or public relations gains or losses to be considered by the owning corporation. Early in the emergence of employee ownership out of conglomerate divestitures, top management of the owning corporation appeared to give little consideration to these matters. The idea that employees might save their jobs through buying the plant then seemed so farfetched that management could rebuff such proposals with little thought of public embarrassment or political pressures. As employee ownership has become more common and has received increasing amounts of publicity, a management concerned with its public image as a socially responsible company can no longer afford to dismiss the possible sale to employees without serious consideration.

TYPES OF LEADERS REQUIRED FOR A BUYOUT

Several different types of leaders are required for a successful employee purchase campaign. In some cases, a single individual may perform two or more of these roles, but it is nevertheless useful to think of them separately in assessing the possibilities of finding the leaders necessary for organizing the campaign (Stern and Hammer 1978). There are three distinct roles important for success in employee or employee-community ownership: a chief executive officer (CEO) capable of providing managerial leadership in production and marketing, a financial expert capable of analyzing financial needs and dealing with sources of funds, and an organizer able to link workers, management people, community leaders, politicians, government officials, and the press in an at least temporary coalition to launch the project.

An able and experienced executive is indispensable for a successful campaign. Banks and government lending agencies are unlikely to approve loans unless they have confidence in the chief executive officer. Furthermore, employees and community people are unlikely to be willing to make financial sacrifices in buying stock unless they have confidence in the prospective manager of the new organization.

In each case of success in buying a plant that we have studied, one or more key management people in the local plant have been willing to cast their lot with the new employee- or employee-community-owned company. While they may have difficulty in adjusting to their executive roles under this new form of ownership, they have at least the advantage of the intimate knowledge of operations. In two cases where no member of management was willing to stay with the plant, the problem of recruiting and appointing a new chief executive officer overwhelmed our efforts to help the local group save the jobs. The problem was supplying all the pieces of the puzzle when the availability of each piece depends upon the presence of the other pieces. Quite apart from the unavoidable risks of taking a job in such a changeover, the prospective CEO is unlikely to consider the position seriously unless he sees that the problems of financing the purchase and providing operating capital have been solved. At the same time, the individuals and organizations counted on for equity or loan capital are not inclined to commit their money until they are persuaded that a competent CEO has accepted the challenge offered.

We have found workers well aware of the need for professional managerial leadership. While they may believe that they could operate the plant with fewer management people than in the past, they recognize that their experience and educational backgrounds have not prepared them to cope with financial, legal, marketing, and engineering problems.

If the prospective CEO does not also have skills and experience in financial analysis and in negotiating with banks and government lending agencies, the project will require a financial expert. If the project is to be financed entirely from stock purchased by employees and by loans, the two roles of managerial leader and financial expert may be sufficient to launch the project. If the project requires substantial investments by community members, the role of organizing entrepreneur is essential. He or she must be someone who can lead a money-raising campaign, bring competing factions within the plant together, and secure the interest and cooperation of public agencies and banks.

In the case of Saratoga Knitting Mill, which was being closed by Cluett-Peabody, Donald Cox played all three roles. The plant was one of sixten that had belonged to VanRaalte Company, a leading firm in the women's undergarment field. The VanRaalte Company had done $70 million of business in 1965. Cluett-Peabody took it over in 1968. As Cox reported, by 1974, the sixteen-plant Van-Raalte division was down to gross sales of $20 million, with an operating loss of $9 million. The Saratoga Springs mill suffered its first loss in decades in 1974 (Cox 1979).

When Cluett-Peabody decided to sell VanRaalte, Donald Cox was vice president for the division and had several months experi-ence as works manager of the Saratoga Springs plant. He was convinced that, under more efficient management and with its modern high-quality machines and skilled workers, the mill had what was necessary for building a viable business. When some of the employees approached him to organize a campaign to buy the plant, after first dismissing the idea, he decided to accept the challenge.

Cox was well qualified by education, experience, and personality to play all three roles: CEO, financier, and organizer. A college graduate in textile engineering, he had built textile machines and was intimately familiar with the engineering and manufacturing side of the business. He had previously been successful as a troubleshooter who was sent into plants to analyze manufacturing, engineering, marketing, and financial problems in order to improve plant performance. Although he had only a few months experience in Saratoga Springs, he had already established good relations with local bankers and political leaders.

Cox himself provided the managerial leadership and worked out the financial plans necessary for the project. He handled relations with Cluett-Peabody, New York State Business Development Corporation, Adirondack Trust Company, Small Business Administration, Meinhard Commercial Corporation, and DuPont Company, the major producer of the yarn used in the knitting machines.

By the time of the ownership transfer in June 1975, employment was down to less than seventy from previous highs of about double that number. Twenty-six employees bought sixty percent of the stock supporting the purchase, with the remaining 40 percent being sold within the community of Saratoga Springs. Cluett-Peabody assisted with a $100,000 loan guarantee, and Cox raised approximately $2 million in loans from public and private sources. Within six months, the new firm, Saratoga Knitting Mill, was earning profits sufficient to justify a bonus to all employees, and the company has continued to be successful in a highly competitive and low profit industry. Saratoga Knitting Mill established an employee stock ownership trust in January 1976, which now holds over 50 percent of company stock, which means also that all the approximately one hundred and forty workers are now owners.

What is now the Mohawk Valley Community Corporation was established in 1876 to produce library furniture, equipment, and supplies. Under the name of Library Bureau it remained independent until 1927. After a series of mergers, Library Bureau came to be owned by Sperry-Rand Corporation in 1955. Although the plant had made a profit during nineteen of the first twenty years of Sperry-Rand ownership, the profits were below the level considered satisfactory by top management. This was also a plant whose products had no relation to the main lines of business for the owning corporation and so was no longer deemed essential to the plans of Sperry-Rand.

In the Library Bureau purchase, the three leadership roles were played by three individuals. When Sperry-Rand announced its shutdown plans, two rival groups stepped forward to try to purchase the plant. One group was headed by men who had substantial management and marketing experience with the Library Bureau but lacked experience in finance. The other group was composed of individuals with ample experience and expertise in financial operations but with no experience in this line of manufacturing and marketing. In this case, the role of the organizing entrepreneur proved indispensable. John Ladd, director of the Mohawk Valley Economic Development District, stepped into the breach and got the two competing parties together, playing the role of mediator until they reached an agreement. At the same time, he was organizing a campaign to raise money through employee stock purchases, stock sales in the surrounding community, and government and bank loans. It was only when these three essential functions meshed that it proved possible to create the employee-community–owned company.

DETERMINING FEASIBILITY

Employee purchase of a plant is necessarily a risky operation. Therefore, anyone providing technical assistance has an obligation to see to it that plans for purchase are supported by a solid feasibility study; and, of course, no lending agency will provide credit unless the proposal is based upon a feasibility study that points to a reasonable chance of success. Even when local people have access to the figures, outside technical assistance is likely to be required. Making of feasibility studies is a rather specialized professional occupation, and potential lending agencies are likely to be more impressed by an outside job by professionals than by an inside product that, objectively, may be of equal quality.

Hiring a consulting firm for a feasibility study may cost the project $50,000 to $100,000, depending upon the problems to be analyzed. In the case of the Mohawk Valley Community Corporation, leaders of the project secured invaluable technical assistance in carrying out the feasibility study through professionals employed by the EDA-supported University Economic Development Center of the State University of New York at Plattsburgh.

When the community is involved in the job-saving campaign, we have found that individuals who may be called free professionals are a very important resource (Stern and Hammer 1978). A century and a half ago, Alexis de Tocqueville remarked upon the importance of voluntarism in American culture. When faced with some community problem, Americans tend to volunteer their ideas and efforts and thus to perform work for which they receive no direct compensation. Visitors from abroad remind us that this strain of voluntarism is still prominent, but in recent decades voluntarism has been largely confined to social service activities. Very little of this voluntarism has so far been channeled into the saving or creating of jobs. Why not? In the past it has been assumed that volunteers should work in the nonprofit sector of the economy and that private enterprise would take care of jobs in the profit sector. Now, when private enterprise has failed to provide the jobs needed or when a shutdown of a privately owned plant threatens to devastate the community, in some cases volunteers have stepped forward to offer expertise. Local lawyers, bankers, accountants, and engineers, as well as religious and political leaders, have volunteered to help the workers and the community meet the shutdown emergency. They offer their time and talents with no concern for immediate material benefits. To be sure, if a local lawyer helps in the conversion to employee ownership, in the future he or she is more likely to get the new company as a client than would other lawyers who have not volunteered their services, but calculation of potential financial gain does not seem to be an important motivation.

Volunteers must be distinguished from those who offer their support contingent on some future material benefit. For example, in the case of the campaign to establish the Mohawk Valley Community Corporation, one man offered to purchase substantial blocks of stock if the company would sign a five-year contract with a warehouse he owned, and two men demanded positions on its board of directors in exchange for stock purchases. Refusing to make any such deals, the organizers of the campaign decided to count on voluntary support and were successful in raising nearly $1.8 million from among 3,550 stock purchasers, with the largest investor putting up $11,000—and this in an area where unemployment was then over 13 percent.

Free professionals may be particularly important in helping the organizing group make what might be called a prefeasibility study. If the project to buy the plant is bound to fail, it is important that those interested in helping workers and community people advise them against trying to raise fifty to a hundred thousand dollars for a full-scale feasibility study. While no preliminary study can take the risk out of a plant purchase, before committing large sums of money it is important to get volunteer service to determine whether there is a realistic possibility of success.

While rank-and-file workers and local union leaders may have less to offer in expertise on marketing, financial, and legal problems than the professionals, their experience and expertise are crucial to the reassessment of the human resources necessary to operate a viable employee-owned plant. In many cases, it will prove impossible to create such a firm without reducing the size of the work force. In one unsuccessful effort to purchase a shutdown plant, the local union leaders planned to reduce by seventy-five the four hundred fifty–person work force employed at the time of the closing. They began by asking the stewards and workers to disregard the staffing arrangements that had prevailed at the time of the plant closing and to simply reflect their own experience and knowledge of production problems and processes in estimating how many workers would be required in that unit in order to produce efficiently.

How could it be that the union could agree to a one-sixth reduction in the work force when the union had always previously insisted more workers were absolutely necessary to operate the plant? The local union president explained that, under the adversarial relationship that prevailed previously, the union was always pushing management to maximize employment. Over a period of years, as disputes arose over job content and work loads, local management often made concessions to keep the peace by adding a job here and a job there. Naturally, management found it much easier to add jobs than to take them away. The union leaders would have preferred to have four hundred fifty jobs rather than three hundred seventy-five, but when the realistic choice was between three hundred seventy-five and zero, they had no difficulty in settling for three hundred seventy-five. Of course, it was necessary to engage in a painstaking discussion and analysis to determine the feasible limit of work force reduction.

It may also be possible to achieve substantial savings in reducing the number of management positions. The potential here is illustrated negatively by a case in which ownership was converted in the opposite direction, from a worker-owned plywood cooperative to a private corporation (Greenberg 1981). One of the first moves that the private company made after taking over the cooperative was to appoint seven additional foremen. In a traditional adversarial relationship between labor and management, a major part of the foreman's responsibilities is to play the role of policeman, to see to it that workers are following orders, are not "goofing off," and are not doing careless work. Hiring a relatively large number of supervisors inevitably gives workers the message that management does not trust them. Where workers feel that the company is really their own, they police themselves to some extent, thus freeing supervisors to serve as trainers, coordinators, and troubleshooters.

Although these potential gains in the reduction of management personnel may be substantial, it is difficult to estimate them in advance. Having had years of experience in a given department, workers can speak authoritatively about which production jobs are necessary and which can be dispensed with. Workers may be almost equally knowledgeable regarding the number of first-line supervisors that will be required. But for higher level management and for staff positions, experience provides workers a less adequate basis of judgment. Therefore, in making the feasibility study it may be prudent to avoid counting on large reductions in management personnel. Project leaders may assume that it will be possible to achieve such reductions in the future, but these will have to be worked out gradually, as workers and management gain experience with the new form of organization.

PUTTING THE PACKAGE TOGETHER

One important source of funds is direct purchase of stock by employees and by members of the community. Although this has provided an essential part of the financing in some cases, such direct purchases will hardly ever be sufficient to provide all the capital needed.

In the past, bankers have been reluctant to lend money to such an unfamiliar entity as an employee-owned firm. As this form of ownership becomes more common, these attitudes seem to be changing, but bankers can still be expected to base their decisions to a large extent upon their assessment of the ability of the prospective chief executive officer. Bankers are also likely to be favorably impressed by a plan to establish an employee stock ownership trust. Not only has this legal and financial instrument been getting increasing publicity around the country, but it tends to increase the probablility that the borrower will be able to repay the loan. Under a conventional loan, the borrower can deduct only the interest payments from company income before paying taxes. With an employee stock ownership plan (ESOP), both interest and principal payments are deductible.

In most cases that occurred in the 1970s, bankers were unwilling to lend all the capital required to finance a project without government participation in the lending program or without government loan guarantees. The Economic Development Administration has been the most active government agency in this field, having provided essential capital in several cases. The money has been provided either as a direct loan to the company or as a component in a grant-loan project in which the money is granted to a city or county development agency, which then lends that money to the emerging company. The company then repays principal and interest, not to the federal government, but to the city or county agency, which thus assumes management of a revolving fund to be used for future industrial development projects. The Urban Development Action Grants (UDAG) Program of the Department of Housing and Urban Development also involves the support of grant-loan projects. So far, UDAG has been used in only one case, but Rath Packing Company is sufficiently important to deserve extended discussion later. The Farmers Home Administration has also supported one large employee ownership conversion through a loan guarantee, that of Bates Manufacturing Company.

Examination of several cases will illustrate some of the financial strategies that have been used, proceeding from the simple to the more complex.

The South Bend Lathe case involved an employee take-over financed completely by an employee stock ownership plan. Here the campaign to purchase the plant was led by works manager Richard Boulis, who became president of the new employee-owned company after its purchase from the conglomerate, Amsted Industries. In this case, the employees did not have to pay cash for any stock. The Economic Development Administration played an essential role in providing $5 million through a grant to the City of South Bend, which in turn lent the money at 3 percent interest to the emerging employee-owned company; $5 million was borrowed at 5 percent above prime from private sources. A complication in this case was that Boulis persuaded the local union leaders that the only way to save their jobs was to abandon the pension program, except for those workers whose pension contributions were already vested, and take employee stock ownership in exchange. This was a painful decision for the local union leaders, and the international officials bitterly opposed it, going to the extent of filing suit to block the abandonment of the pension program.

In the case of Saratoga Knitting Mill, Donald Cox began the money-raising campaign with an employee meeting, during which he proposed that the employees get together to buy the plant and pledged $10,000 of personal monies to start the campaign. Workers then made financial commitments. In some cases, this involved mortgaging homes and borrowing money from relatives or financial institutions. Cox then raised 40 percent of the equity capital needed from community investors. In this case, there was no communitywide campaign. Cox simply called upon several prominent citizens to persuade them to invest. He also led the campaign to raise substantial loan money from private and public sources.

The Mohawk Valley Community Corporation case involves the broadest communitywide campaign on which we have information. Organizers of the campaign had considerable difficulties at the outset in persuading management of Sperry-Rand to negotiate a sale rather than simply shutting the plant down and selling its equipment. When management finally agreed to consider a sale to employees, Sperry-Rand required a nonrefundable deposit of $200,000 to test the seriousness of their interest. Mohawk Valley Economic Development District director John Ladd conferred with local managment poeple and with leaders of the white-collar and blue-collar workers' locals of the International Union of Electrical, Radio, and Machine Workers. They arranged for a meeting to present this challenge to all employees at a local high school. With the full cooperation of the local union leaders, the organizers were able to raise $193,000 within several days. Sperry-Rand officials then agreed that this was sufficient to keep the deal open.

When Ladd had secured an agreement of the rival management groups seeking to take over the plant, the organizers of the campaign mapped out their financial strategy. They would seek to borrow $2 million from banks in the area, giving the banks a first mortgage on plant and equipment. They would ask EDA to provide an additional $2 million in loan money, in effect taking a second mortgage. This meant that even if the firm went bankrupt, its assets would be well over $2 million, so the banks could hardly lose. The organizers also proposed to raise approximately $1.75 million in stock.

One of the problems in such a money-raising program is that each component of the package is contingent on the other two. That is, EDA would not provide the loan without the equity money and commitments from the banks, and the bankers would make their commitments only on the assumption that the other components were in place. Also, of course, the organizing group could not put on a stock-selling campaign without prior assurance that the two sources of loan money were secured. Ladd approached three banks in the area to tell them that they were going to have an opportunity to share among them $2 million in loan money. While the bankers were surprised by this proposal, they had already had a record of successful dealings with Ladd in financing profitable private business enterprises, and he was able to persuade them to make the commitment.

The leaders of the campaign recognized that, with a total work force of about two hundred sixty, it would be impossible to come close to raising the equity money required from the sale of stock to employees only, so a communitywide campaign was called for. The organizers decided on a strategy of seeking a large number of small stockholders rather than trying to finance the purchase through large volume stock purchases by a few wealthy individuals.

The organizers then sought to register the stock offering with the Securities and Exchange Commission, but found this was impossible without a statement from Sperry-Rand guaranteeing the accuracy of the plant financial figures. While local management people had all the figures needed for a solid feasibility study, only the current owners of the plant could guarantee those figures. Perhaps being concerned about legal liabilities if the employee-owned firm later failed, Sperry-Rand management declined to give this guarantee.

This meant that the stock could be sold only within New York State and would require approval from the state attorney general for such a stock offering. This was a serious handicap since it ruled out purchases by plant sales personnel located in other states.

Meeting with the attorney general, the organizers not only secured his approval in principle but also gained an extraordinary degree of cooperation from his office. One of his assistants worked constantly with the organizing group over a period of several weeks, going over the brochure describing the stock issue and reviewing and approving all of the news media releases and radio and television advertising. The planners of the campaign decided to price the stock at $2 a share and to make the minimum purchase 100 shares and the maximum purchase 12,500 shares. As it turned out the largest stock purchaser invested $11,000 for 5,500 shares.

Ladd and his associates organized the stock sales campaign like a United Way drive. They had leading bankers and business and professional people on their committee. They divided the territory geographically and in terms of occupational groups, setting targets for money to be raised in each area and also, in the cases of potential large investors, estimating how many shares of stock each one should be asked to purchase.

All of this effort had to be carried out within a forty-five-day period, since Sperry-Rand had allowed only that much time to complete the deal. The organizers launched the campaign with a media blitz—news stories, radio and TV interviews, and paid announcements. Brokers in the area agreed to sell the stock without commission. Before the end of the forty-five days, the sales campaign had brought in 3,550 investors in an area with over 13 percent unemployment at the time. Thirty-four percent of the stock was purchased within the new company, the remaining almost two-thirds being raised from community supporters.

In this case the analogy with the United Way campaign seems particularly apt. Most of the 3,550 investors had never purchased stock before. In fact, many of them had only a vague idea of the meaning of the stock purchases: that they had a right to vote for members of the board of directors, that they would eventually receive dividends if the company was successful, and so on. In other words, purchasers did not see themselves as investing but rather as making contributions to the welfare of the workers and the community.

In the cases described so far, local unions simply followed the lead of local management people or community leaders in cooperating to save their jobs, and higher level union officials seemed to be confused and ambivalent. The next chapter will present cases in which local union officials took the lead in organizing the job-saving campaign.

DECIDING ON THE LEGAL STRUCTURE

In deciding on the legal structure for a reorganized firm, planners should think beyond the immediate needs of raising money to cover the purchase price and to provide operating capital. If they are interested in more than the immediate saving of the jobs, they need to think also of the different long-run consequences of the various options for legal structure.

Since few workers have had any experience with stock ownership, in the crisis of an impending plant shutdown, they are likely to accept any legal structure proposed to them by a local lawyer. The lawyer will almost certainly propose a traditional stock ownership arrangement, which provides for one vote for each share of stock and which makes no provision for the establishment of a stock trust that would allow worker voting power to be pooled. When this arrangement prevails, workers are almost certain to lose their predominant ownership and potential control over the company over time, and this can happen even within a few months.

With the traditional stock ownership arrangement, workers find themselves in a catch-22. They can lose control of the company either if it fails, in which case there is no company to control, or if it is highly successful. In the latter case, as production expands and new workers are hired, the original worker-owners will recognize that selling stock to new employees will dilute their equity in the firm, and so what might be called collective selfishness takes over. The firm comes to be made up of two classes of people: worker-owners and hired labor. This development tends to undermine the sense of collective purpose and weaken worker motivation to contribute to the progress of the firm. As worker-owners reach retirement, they are of course glad to sell to nonowning workers, but by this time the value of the stock may have increased so greatly as to take it out of the reach of the more recently hired workers. If so, retiring worker-owners have no option except to sell stock to outsiders, and the firm gradually reverts to the traditional form of private ownership.

This reversion has occurred even in the well-known plywood cooperatives, which have been so firmly based upon egalitarian principles that everyone except the hired manager receives the same hourly pay and everyone has only one share of stock, thus providing for one-worker-one-vote in the early stages of the life of the firm. In some of these cases, as the firm has become highly successful and the value of the stock has correspondingly increased, the original worker-owners have succumbed to collective selfishness, taking in new people only as hired labor. By the time worker-owners were ready to retire, the value of a single share of their stock increased so much as to make it beyond the reach of the workers hired after the initial stock sale, so the retiring worker-owners sold to outsiders. In this way, several plywood cooperatives have become absentee-owned firms.

Byers Transport Limited, based in Edmonton, Alberta, provides an example in which the long-term ownership of the employees is protected through an unusual stock purchase program. Byers had originally been a privately owned company and was later taken over by an airline. When the airline was taken over by the government, the policy makers decided it was not appropriate for government to own a trucking company. While the government was considering plans for Byers, the firm's chief executive officer organized a campaign for employee ownership. Stock sales were limited to employees, and nearly all of them bought shares. Forty-four percent of the shares were bought by rank-and-file workers and 9 percent by first-line supervisors, thus providing the two lowest levels of the company a majority. In order to avoid increasing concentration of stock at higher company levels, the designers of the plan adopted a rule that an employee could sell only to another employee at the same organizational level or to the company, which would then be required to offer it to an employee in the same category as the worker who sold to the company. Since there would be no public market for stock owned entirely by employees, management established an accounting system to fix share prices in terms of book value and company earnings. Under this system, the buying and selling of stock does not change the percentages held within the four organizational levels.

Another option is to structure the firm as a worker cooperative, with only full-time workers being members and each member having a single vote, as in consumer cooperatives and other types of cooperative organizations. In order to avoid the gradual conversion of the cooperative into an absentee-owned firm, it is necessary to write into its constitution provisions that guarantee access to ownership on an equal basis to new workers and that maintain the price of the stock or other ownership instrument at a level within reach of those new workers. This will assure that control of the firm is based upon labor rather than upon capital, even if the right to vote is legally based on an individual stock certificate (Ellerman 1980).

As David Ellerman has pointed out, in order to maintain a cooperative organization legally based on stock ownership, it is important to recognize that traditionally stock certificates have embodied two sets of rights: voting rights and rights to share in the capital and earnings of the company (Ellerman 1980). To maintain a democratically controlled organization, it is important to keep separate the legal instruments establishing these rights. This can be done through issuing two classes of stock. Voting rights could be limited to class A stock, with the provision that only workers could purchase such stock and that each worker would have only one share. Class B, or nonvoting, stock would fluctuate in value in relation to earnings and the net worth of the company. Such stock could be sold to outsiders without jeopardizing employee control. Class B stock could also be purchased in unlimited amounts by employees, and shares could be distributed annually in relation to earnings.

Today, the most popular form of employee ownership is based upon the employee stock ownership trust, a legal entity supported by federal ESOP legislation first introduced by Senator Russell Long in 1974. Although the sponsors of the original legislation were interested in simply broadening ownership in established firms so that more employees would feel they had a stake in firm performance, the ESOP has been increasingly used to save jobs in impending plant shutdowns.

Until recently, leaders of organized labor have been highly critical of ESOPs, arguing that they are useful primarily to management in providing access to new capital on more favorable terms than the market offers and that they give workers the illusion of sharing in ownership when they actually have no influence on decision making. While this criticism fits many cases, critics of the ESOP have failed to recognize that it is a highly flexible legal instrument. As one of the leading ESOP lawyers, Norman Kurland argues, the nature of the ESOP depends primarily upon the motivations and interests of the individual or group that sets it up. That is, it is possible to design an ESOP in which workers receive only nonvoting stock. If the stock appears to carry voting rights, management can structure the arrangement so that the board of directors selects the initial trustees who vote the stock held by the trust and thus can continue to reelect those currently in control.

On the other hand, even when stock is unevenly distributed within the work force, it is possible to establish an ESOP on a highly democratic basis. The trustees can be elected on a one-worker-one-vote basis, and then the trustees are, of course, able to vote for members of the board of directors as instructed by the majority of the workers. In other words, the existence of the employee stock ownership trust makes possible consolidation of worker voting power. This is the model adopted by Rath Packing Company. It should be noted, however, that under current legislation, the stock trust can only be maintained for five years, after which the stock must be distributed to the individual worker-owners. Unless new legislation makes it possible upon a vote of employee-owners to maintain the trust for a longer period, the ESOP cannot provide any long-run guarantee of retention of employee ownership and control.

While noting the problems inherent in the ESOP from the standpoint of workers or union leaders interested in maintaining employee ownership and worker participation in management, an ESOP's potential financial advantages to both workers and companies should not be overlooked. In some cases, Bates Manufacturing and South Bend Lathe, for example, workers gain ownership without paying for the stock. The transaction is based on the company's future earnings. Even if workers pay for the stock through payroll deductions, in the case of a profitable company, as Corey Rosen of the National Center for Employee Ownership points out in a personal communication, $20 set aside for worker stock purchase will cost a company in the 46 percent tax bracket only $11. "The point . . . is," Rosen adds, "That this is the way people who already have wealth raise more of it—in pre-tax dollars through borrowing and other sheltering devices. Why shouldn't workers be able to do the same?"

OTHER RESOURCES AND CONSULTANTS

Readers should recognize that ESOPs and other employee ownership plans involve complex and technical legal and financing problems. We have attempted only a preliminary orientation, for the purpose of helping people to recognize that there is a variety of options to be considered in any move toward employee ownership. Those seeking further and more detailed information and guidance should consult other sources, such as those listed at the back of the book.

In referring to consultants in an impending plant shutdown situation, what should a client organization expect? Consultants should not be expected to *sell* employee ownership or worker participation. If local people see prospects of attracting a private buyer committed to operating the plant rather than liquidating it, this outcome would obviously be less risky than attempting to solve the complex legal, financial, and organizational problems involved in employee ownership. Since, however, experience so far suggests that the private buyer solution is often based on a community's wishful thinking, we advise local people to begin exploring the employee ownership option even as they actively pursue private investors.

While our own values favor worker participation in management, and we have cited cases where the lack of such participation has led to conflict in employee-owned firms, in a shutdown crisis, leaders of workers, management, and community may be so preoccupied with the problem of saving jobs that they regard questions of worker participation as needless digressions. Furthermore, they may believe that potential sources of credit will be less likely to lend money to a democratically managed firm. Or, if organizers are prepared to accept a CEO who is highly competent in production and marketing in their particular industry but who has no interest in worker participation, we do not urge them to go find a leader who favors participatory methods but who may have much less mastery of the technical side of the business. We do, nevertheless, think it appropriate for consultants to work with both the potential CEO and worker representatives to help them to recognize that managing an employee-owned business is not the same as managing a private company.

At the New Systems of Work and Participation Program, Cornell University, we see our role as helping people in the field to recognize that there are various options in structuring an employee-owned company and various styles of management and worker participation. It is certainly appropriate for consultants to help members of the client organization to explore these options. While we take pains to leave decisions in the hands of those who will have to live with them, we do seek to provide information and ideas that will enable them to make informed decisions.

5.
The Union and
the Transition to
Employee Ownership

Robert N. Stern, William Foote Whyte, Tove Hammer, and Christopher B. Meek

THE EMERGENCE OF employee ownership from plant shutdowns in the 1970s took union leaders by surprise. This dramatic shift in ownership presented unions with new potentials but also with new problems. At first, union leaders at the level of the international were naturally more concerned with problems than with potentials. Now, as they have had a few years more experience with this new phenomenon, they are beginning to appreciate the potentials, but the shift still presents them with problems for which they have been largely unprepared.

How do union leaders view employee ownership? To answer that question, we have to distinguish between local union officers and the union policy makers in the central offices. Until well into the decade of the 1970s, when faced with the choice between employee ownership and unemployment, local union leaders uniformly responded to appeals from local management and community leaders to join in the campaign to save the jobs. During this period, the attitudes of higher level union officials can be best described as ambivalent. They could hardly say that they preferred to have their members unemployed rather than to become worker-owners, but the apparent contradiction between collective bargaining and employee ownership immobilized them. They generally provided little assistance to local officers in working out the new ownership arrangement. By 1980, as international union officials became more familiar with employee ownership, their attitudes shifted toward a willingness to consider employee buy-outs as one option in meeting a possible plant shutdown.

SOURCES OF NEGATIVE UNION ATTITUDES

Six factors seem to underlie negative reactions of union leaders to employee ownership: historical experience, differences between locals and internationals, worker risk, worry about undermining the traditional adversarial relationship between labor and management, distrust of the ESOP, and fear of the unknown. The analysis here is based primarily on the data from a survey carried out in 1977 by Robert Stern and Rae Anne O'Brien. The researchers obtained responses from 49 presidents or research or education directors of international unions, 35 percent of the 140 international unions to which the questionnaire was mailed. In many cases, the respondents wrote detailed comments in addition to checking off items that indicated their attitudes on particular questions.

Historical Experience. As Aldrich and Stern (1983) have noted in their extensive historical study of worker cooperatives in the United States, until late in the nineteenth century many union leaders had highly favorable attitudes toward employee ownership and worker cooperatives. Furthermore, when they were locked out by their employers in a labor dispute, they sometimes responded by forming their own cooperative firm. In some cases, these worker cooperatives were successful to the extent of forcing management to settle with the union and bring the craftsmen back to work. That is, the worker cooperative was successful as a strike strategy, but ceased to exist upon a successful conclusion of the strike. Particularly in times of periodic depressions, Aldrich and Stern have found upsurges of worker cooperative or employee-owned firms, but the formal stance of the union movement toward worker cooperatives was determined in early conventions of the American Federation of Labor during which leaders of the movement pushed through resolutions endorsing collective bargaining as the basic union strategy and thereby dismissing worker cooperatives. Because few of these employee-owned firms organized in earlier periods have survived for many years, this history has colored the views of some top union officers. For example, one official responded to the questionnaire with this comment: "Many years ago [our union] encouraged the development of employee-owned enterprises as a method of bringing strikes to a conclusion or an attempt through cooperative programs of promoting employment. All eventually failed." Such negative evaluation of past experience naturally promotes skepticism toward renewed efforts to save jobs through employee ownership.

Interest Differences between Locals and Internationals. Local union officers naturally concentrate on maintaining jobs and good working conditions. While the high-level officials share these objectives, they are also concerned with maintaining the standards they won over the years in negotiating companywide and even industrywide master contracts. Traditionally, union leaders have sought to extend the scope of coverage of the basic contract so as to avoid the kind of competition among locals that would tend to undermine the international union. That is, it may be in the interests of workers in a given local to accept a wage freeze or even a pay cut if such sacrifices are necessary to save their jobs. Higher level officials may not be able to prevent local unions from negotiating such sacrifices, but those cases pose severe problems for the international. The top union leaders recognize that, if they go along with wage and benefit concessions for one plant, they can expect management in the same company to try to make the same case for worker sacrifices in other plants. They can also expect to get pressure for similar sacrifices from managements in other companies, supported by the argument that the company in question cannot fairly compete with a firm that has been conceded lower labor costs.

The issue has come up most dramatically in the case of pensions. It has been a long struggle for the major international unions to achieve substantial pension plans for their members, and top union leaders view with alarm any management move to reduce or eliminate pension rights. It was this issue that provoked the split between the local and the top officials of the United Steelworkers of America in the South Bend Lathe case. Works manager Richard Boulis argued that it would be impossible to maintain jobs under employee ownership unless the workers were willing to exchange their pension plan for employee stock ownership. He also argued that this exchange could lead to the workers getting more money in the long run than they were sacrificing. International officials adamantly opposed the surrender of the pension plan and sued to force the company to restore the plan. When the local union officers were persuaded to accept the exchange, this provoked a conflict between local and international, which culminated in a decertification election. While the workers voted by a narrow margin to retain their union membership, the memories of this struggle are still fresh in the top offices of the United Steelworkers and in union circles generally.

Worker Risk. Concern for worker risk is a more general formulation of the issue discussed in the South Bend Lathe exchange of a pension program for employee stock ownership. By law, pension funds must be invested in a variety of securities, with no more than 10 percent being invested in the company of the employer, except as provided by ESOP legislation. While the federal government provides a guarantee of pension funds in case the company cannot meet its obligations, no such guarantee is provided under employee stock ownership. Bankruptcy of the company can render the employee-owned stock worthless. When the employee ownership project requires workers to purchase stock out of their own savings, union leaders are naturally concerned about this concentration of risk. Such an arrangement means that, if the company fails, workers lose not only their jobs but whatever savings they have invested.

Attachment to the Traditional Adversarial Relationship. When employees come to own the company, the union finds itself in an unprecedented position. This is frequently expressed with the question, "How can you bargain with yourself?" The Stern-O'Brien survey (1977) elicited the following comments from leaders in the international offices:

Under such circumstances, labor's traditional functions in this economy are changed dramatically if not eliminated.

. . .Employee ownership of a production facility would probably have a negative effect on the union. It would seem that the group loyalty would be switched to an interest in the success of the company rather than collective bargaining.

. . .serious identity crisis . . . .

. . .minefield for collective bargaining.

If there is no employer, why kid ourselves about the union?

Distrust of the ESOP. In their first encounters with ESOPs, union leaders were inclined to view the instrument as only a device to help management raise capital. They also saw the threat to the union as some managements might try to give the workers the illusion of ownership (without any real power) and thus weaken their commitment to the union.

Fear of the Unknown. Stern has likened union leaders' fear of the unknown to the old story of the song of the canary. Miners used to take a caged canary with them into underground mines to test for the presence of poisonous or explosive gas. If the bird died, it warned miners of gas leaks, and its sacrifice provided a signal for the miners to get out of the mine. Union leaders had great anxieties about playing the role of the canary in this uncharted field. They were inclined to take a cautious wait-and-see attitude—let others try employee ownership first, and see how they fare. We found union leaders hoping that the issue of employee ownership would not be forced upon their own union until they had a chance to observe how other unions had fared under this new arrangement.

In the early stages of the development of employee ownership, these attitudes and perceptions at the top levels of unions led the international officers to play passive roles. This necessarily left the initiative in the hands of local people. Furthermore, getting no guidance from higher level officials, local union officers tended to follow the lead of any local management people who claimed they were trying to save the jobs through employee ownership. With the initiative entirely in management hands, local union leaders were ready to do whatever local managers or community leaders suggested was necessary to save the jobs. Typically, when the employee ownership possibility suddenly arose, workers had already assumed that they were about to become unemployed. Being so fixed on the need to save jobs, they tended to show no interest in questions of long-run maintenance of ownership or of sharing in control of the firm. Before the transfer of ownership, workers typically have only vague expectations as to what the change will mean in day-to-day life in the plant (Hammer and Stern 1980). They make no demands for worker participation in decision making, but they do assume that, somehow, when they become owners they will be treated with more dignity by management and their views will be more respected.

These attitudes and beliefs reported by Stern and O'Brien in 1977 appear to have prevailed among international union officials through the mid-1970s. We now have evidence of marked changes in top-level union orientation in response to more recent experience. These changes are documented by an unpublished study carried out about three years after the Stern-O'Brien survey at Harvard by Doug Kruse and Eric Asard, under the direction of Joseph Blasi. Both surveys covered similar populations of international union presidents or heads of research or education; 49 officers responded in the first survey and 42 in the latter. The questions asked were not identical but similar enough to permit useful comparison. Regarding a general evaluation of employee ownership, 75 percent of the respondents in the 1977 survey took a position classified as "basically negative." In the 1980 survey only 29 percent of the respondents gave a negative reaction to any and all forms of employee ownership, whereas the remaining respondents indicated that there were forms of employee ownership that they could approve.

Comparison of the two surveys also indicates that the union leaders had gained more information and ideas about employee ownership between the two survey periods. In 1977, 15 percent of the respondents ventured no opinion at all. In the 1980 survey, only about 5 percent ventured no opinion. An additional 15 percent expressed a negative evaluation of a specific form of employee ownership, and their responses gave no indication of whether they would approve of any other form.

Perhaps even more striking is the 1980 survey's comparison of the responses of international officers whose locals had had some experience with employee ownership with those international officers who had no such experience. In the case of internationals without any direct experience with employee ownership, 40 percent of the respondents expressed unqualified resistance to any such form. In international unions where one or more locals had been involved with employee ownership, no respondents expressed flat disapproval, and the remaining respondents accepted employee ownership with varying degrees of qualifications. It is also interesting that those venturing no opinion whatsoever or stating objections to one specific form and not making clear their positions on alternatives were entirely confined to unions where there had been no direct experience with employee ownership. All these findings make it clear that there has been a major shift in union attitudes. Increasing union experience with employee ownership has fostered an increasing openness to experimenting with such ownership shifts.

RESPONSE TO OWNERSHIP: FROM EUPHORIA TO ALIENATION

In these early cases emerging under management initiative, we have observed three stages in the development of the relationship:

1. Worker and union solidarity with management in the struggle to save the jobs during the weeks immediately preceeding the ownership conversion.

2. General euphoria when the goal is reached and in the early months of experience with employee ownership. During this period, local union leaders enjoy the opportunities of participating with management people in seminars and other public discussions in which they tell their success story. It is now evident to observers that the parties are working together in a spirit of harmony and mutual respect and trust.

3. Disillusionment as labor relations lapse into the previous adversarial pattern. This stage seems to begin within a year after the conversion to employee ownership. The people who previously managed the plant have now become top management. They are naturally preoccupied with their new and expanded responsibilities.

During the second stage, labor relations are harmonious, so management people have unconsciously made the assumption that the change in ownership requires no change in labor relations or in the style of administering the plant. But workers become increasingly concerned with the apparent contradiction between sharing in ownership and being excluded from any influence in decision making.

The nature of the shift from the first to the third stages can be illustrated by reviewing the history of three employee-owned companies. A month after the dramatic success of their job-saving campaign, four key people from the Mohawk Valley Community Corporation spoke at a seminar at Cornell. Union and management leaders spoke with pride about their joint achievement and made clear the faith they had in each other. When asked whether his management had made any plans for involving worker participation in decision making, the company president shook his head, replying, "We haven't got around to that yet." After a pause he added, "Maybe we should install a suggestion box."

Fifteen months later, when the same cast of characters spoke at a seminar, Whyte met privately with the presidents of the blue- and white-collar workers' unions before the session to ask how things were going. The president of the white-collar union replied, "You ask any worker what it means to work in that plant now. They'll tell you, 'I've got a job.' That's all. Nothing else has changed. This place doesn't run any different now than it did when Sperry-Rand owned it." The president of the blue-collar workers union confirmed this general interpretation and added that his union at that time had five grievances ready to go to arbitration, an extraordinary number for a small plant.

In later contacts with workers and union leaders over a period of months, we found them experiencing increasing dissatisfaction in their relations with management. They also pointed out to us again and again gross inefficiencies in the production operations that they could correct if management were interested in discussing these problems with them. After a very successful year financially (1976–77), Mohawk Valley Community Corporation had run into some serious reverses, which led to a cutting of expenses and reduction of the work force. At one point, it was down close to 100 from a pre–take-over figure of about 260. This decline cannot be blamed exclusively on the lack of any effective utilization of the brains of the workers. Still, the workers are convinced that the company would be in better shape if they had some input into decision making.

The company seems clearly on the road back to traditional private ownership. Four members of management recently purchased enough newly issued shares to give themselves 50 percent of the voting stock and therefore absolute control.

In the case of Vermont Asbestos Group (VAG), the hero of the job-saving campaign was John Lupien, the maintenance supervisor, who rallied workers and a few local townspeople and secured the assistance of the state agencies in negotiating the purchase of the mine from GAF. Initially, over 80 percent of the stock was owned by members of the work force, and each of the 170-odd workers bought at least one fifty-dollar share. John Lupien became chairman of the VAG board, whose membership was evenly divided, with seven rank-and-file workers balanced by seven white-collar workers or members of management. A former mine worker, then a representative in the state legislature, became the fifteenth member.

The ownership and control structure was designed by a local lawyer, Andrew Fields. Neither Fields nor Lupien had any notions of creating economic democracy. Fields described himself as "a little to the right of Barry Goldwater." He believed devoutly in the private enterprise system, and therefore he boasted that he had tried to set up a structure of ownership and control as close to the private enterprise model as possible. When asked about worker participation in management, John Lupien had a stock answer: "If you own stock in General Motors, that doesn't give you the right to run General Motors."

While the composition of the board of directors appeared to give workers a substantial share of power, worker members found themselves in an awkward position. Having been elected by their fellow union members, they assumed that they would be responsible to those members and would be reporting to them regarding the deliberations of the board. To the contrary, Fields informed them that all the board's deliberations must be held strictly confidential, and nothing could be communicated by the worker members to other workers. All communication from the board to the workers would be through official bulletins. Workers were naturally curious regarding salaries that their company was paying members of management. Lupien and the company president at first flatly refused to give out any figures. At this point, lawyer Fields informed them that his interpretation of the law indicated that they could not withhold such information from the worker-stockholders. Even then, top management did not give specific figures. The board finally released figures on *salary ranges*, avoiding pinpointing particular salaries.

At first, VAG was fantastically profitable because shortly after the transfer of ownership, the price of asbestos jumped by 63 percent. Within a year, the workers got back more in dividends than they had paid for the stock. Nevertheless, they were not completely satisfied with the situation, as they began to encounter cases in which top management made major decisions without consulting them, or, in one case, in direct violation of the expressed opinions of the majority of those worker-owners. The action that precipitated the sharpest cleavage between worker-owners and management involved Vermont Industrial Products (VIP), a brainchild of John Lupien, who believed the future of the company depended upon its ability to use asbestos tailings (waste) in the manufacture of asbestos board. Since banks were not inclined to put up much money for this purpose, the project could be financed only out of profits. Management's call for a special meeting of stockholders gave workers the impression that their vote would decide the matter. They did indeed vote and solidly defeated the proposal. Then Fields clarified the situation by explaining that such a vote was only advisory to the board of directors and that the board had the legal right to make its own decision on the matter. Lupien then persuaded the board to authorize the project.

It is important to note that this was not a situation where the workers were shortsightedly preferring immediate income over the the long-term strengthening of the firm. To be sure, the area where asbestos was currently being mined was estimated to run out in about seven years, whereas the tailings, already piled far above the plant, could sustain the proposed VIP for decades. Workers opposing Lupien, however, pointed out that in an area adjoining the mine and owned by the company, geological studies had indicated that there was a fifty-year supply of asbestos. To reach this new source of ore would require substantial excavations, costing millions of dollars. When they expected that the major financing for the VIP proposal would be supplied by a bank, some workers said that they had been willing to go along. When the bankers declined to provide such credit, the workers took this as evidence that the VIP project was unwise. There is no need to render a final judgment on the economic soundness of the VIP plan. The important issue is the way that the decision was made.

When Howard Manosh, a respected local entrepreneur, became aware of the spreading dissatisfaction among the workers and stepped forward with a tender offer of $1,834 for each share originally bought at $50, he was able in a short time to pick up about 30 percent of the shares. In a proxy contest with Lupien's board of directors, Manosh won fourteen out of fifteen seats and took control. The hero of the job-saving campaign at VAG, John Lupien, was then forced out of the company.

When newspapers reported the Manosh takeover, many critics of employee ownership concluded that the case demonstrated that American workers were interested only in money and did not care about ownership. Obviously, if the workers had been offered less money for their stock, they would have been less likely to sell. But the circumstances of the case by no means prove that they were indifferent to ownership. Having discovered through experience that ownership of a large majority of the shares gave them no influence over major decisions affecting their jobs and their lives, they made a rational judgment that the stock had only financial value and that therefore they should get as much money out of it as possible. Union leaders did not seek to discourage such sales to a private investor.

In the South Bend Lathe case, our information comes from correspondence, one conversation with president Richard Boulis, and media accounts. But South Bend Lathe so clearly fits the pattern we are describing as to justify generalizing on the basis of fragmentary information.

South Bend Lathe is one of the most publicized cases of em-

ployee ownership yet to appear, and until recently it had been
extraordinarily successful financially. In this conglomerate divesti-
ture case, 100 percent of the stock is coming to be owned by
employees through an ESOP. Since he appointed the trustees who
vote the stock, Boulis has been firmly in control.

Our first contact with South Bend Lathe was through a letter
Whyte wrote to Boulis, expressing interest in his case. In his
answer, Boulis closed with a sentence that has become one of our
favorite quotations: "We tell our people that they have all the advantages of ownership without any of the headaches of management." We wondered how long it would be before the workers
would begin agitating for a share in those headaches.

Boulis blames the 1980 strike on the union, particularly because its higher officers have never forgiven him and the local for
trading the pension plan in on an ESOP. According to the newspaper and magazine reports, the union leaders have an entirely
different interpretation, which is far more compatible with what
we have seen in similar cases elsewhere. Warren Brown, writing in
the *Washington Post* (September 30, 1980), quotes a young machin-
ist, who had played an important role in persuading workers to
accept the ESOP:

> "What we have had there for the last five years is ownership
> without control. . . . We've bent over backwards since 1975
> to make a good product and keep it selling . . . we've kept
> our mouths shut—covered up our differences with manage-
> ment to avoid publicity. . . .
>
> "But all we got was the same treatment we had before the
> ESOP, maybe even worse. We make no decisions. We have
> no voice, we're owners in name only."

According to Boulis, "Employee ownership does not mean employee management. Somebody has to give the orders to make
things happen. You can't run a business by committee."

Do South Bend Lathe workers want to run the company? The
Post reporter could not find anyone who expressed himself in that
way. He gave this interpretation of the prevailing sentiments:
"None said he wanted to manage the firm, per se. But they all said
that they expected ownership conferred on them a kind of collegial
equality with management in which their opinions would be lis-

tened to, their views sought." The *Post* reporter closed his article with Boulis reporting on what he had learned. He said that, when the strike ended, he was going to try

> "to improve internal communications. When we bought this company, I didn't have time for human relations. I didn't have time to go around patting people on their butts. . . . I didn't think about anything except keeping this business going and making money. But now, maybe I'll find some time for human relations. I guess I'll have to."

At the time, Boulis's self-criticism was limited to his failure to develop friendly relations with individual workers.

In an effort to respond constructively to the strike, Boulis reported in a personal communication, several months later he worked out with union leaders a program called "share circles," apparently an adaptation of the Japanese quality control circles. More recently, however, management has been moving more along the traditional lines of private industry, acquiring two other companies in the United States and establishing a joint venture in South Korea. Management states that its standard model, which the Korean firm will manufacture, can no longer be produced domestically at a profit and that technically more advanced models are being developed for the South Bend plant. In any case, employment at South Bend was down sharply in 1982, and the workers, while recognizing the effects of the recession on jobs, are naturally wondering to what extent *their* company is exporting *their* jobs to Korea. In a situation where workers have no influence over basic management decisions, such anxieties may be inevitable.

Another case, on which we have only fragmentary information, so clearly fits the emerging pattern as to be worth mention. Okonite Company, after many years as a successful independent firm, manufacturing copper and steel cables, was taken over by a conglomerate. When the conglomerate went into bankruptcy, workers, community leaders, and politicians in New Jersey, the headquarters of the Okonite Division, made extraordinary efforts to save the jobs of an important firm that had always been profitable, even through the conglomerate years. The saving of about eighteen hundred jobs was accomplished by a plan that involved employee stock ownership supported by large sums from EDA as a grant to the state job development authority, which lent the money to the company, and by substantial loans from private banks. The instrument of ownership was nonvoting stock. When we spoke to the vice president of industrial relations early in the development of this new employee ownership case, he commented, "Really, the banks own us." Apparently workers have come to the same conclusion. In the spring of 1981, an Okonite plant with 290 workers went through a twelve-week strike. When the local president was asked how the workers could strike against the company they owned, he flatly denied that they really owned the company.

In general, blue-collar workers have had no experience in ownership of stock. When they do receive stock indicating that they share in ownership of their own company, they tend to interpret ownership in terms familiar to them, as it applies to personal possessions such as a house or a car. They are not familiar with the separation of control from ownership. When they do experience this separation, they become concerned about the apparent contradiction between sharing in ownership and being barred from sharing in making decisions about the management of their company.

When the legal and structural aspects of employee ownership are established by management, the union remains in its traditional reactive role. When the union sets the pattern for employee ownership, however, this necessarily changes the roles of union leaders, workers, and management people and presents them with a new set of problems and potentials.

These new roles are likely to arise under more adverse economic conditions than those facing the management-controlled transformations of the 1970s. Management people are most likely to take the initiative in cases where the plant being divested has been making profits or where local managers are convinced that local losses have been caused by mistaken decisions and policies imposed by remote control and that local autonomy will assure future profits. If the plant has been sustaining serious losses for some years, management people are less likely to see the potential for economic revival under employee ownership. Since they usually have good prospects of being transferred to management positions elsewhere within the company, they are naturally reluctant to risk their jobs by taking command of what appears to be a sinking ship.

The situation is quite different for workers and local union leaders. They may not be highly optimistic on the prospects for success under employee ownership, but workers have fewer and less attractive job alternatives than managers. A shutdown will mean extended unemployment for most of them. Those who find jobs locally are almost certain to start with wages and benefits substantially below their previous level. Leaving the area for jobs elsewhere means disrupting family and friendship ties as well as having to sell a home in a depressed housing market.

How can unions meet this twofold challenge of establishing new roles for workers, union leaders, and managers while building a social system to gain major improvements in productivity that will assure the long-term survival of the new company? This general question can be broken down into more specific questions.

Suppose workers and union leaders seek not only to save the jobs for the immediate future but also to maintain control of the company for the long run. How do they solve the complex financial, legal, and social design problems necessary to support this long-term objective?

How does the union structure the board of directors so as to ensure expertise needed to win the confidence of potential funding sources and also to provide strong guidance for management, without abandoning its long-run control objectives? Can the new board of directors secure a chief executive officer who has the superior abilities needed and is willing to confront the risks involved in leading a firm in a precarious financial position with such an unfamiliar pattern of power sharing?

How can local union leaders develop relations with the international so as to receive guidance and support, or at least to avoid destructive conflict between local and international? Can the local union maintain its adversarial relationship with the company in grievance handling and bargaining while at the same time cooperating with management in increasing productivity?

How can union and management work together in securing worker and supervisor participation in building a system of cooperative problem solving to increase productivity?

UNION INITIATIVE: THE LANDMARK CASE OF RATH PACKING COMPANY

The leaders of union and management at Rath Packing Company have had to try to answer all these questions. While they may not have devised the best possible answers, since they have dealt resourcefully with these questions, the story of their experience can provide useful guidance for those moving into the territory in the future. Of course, there is no one best way to answer any of these questions. For any new case, the answers must be adapted to the current economic situation and the existing state of union-management relations. But a knowledge of the Rath case can help prospective leaders of new projects to anticipate problems and to consider options that otherwise might not have occurred to them.

Founded early in the twentieth century as a family business, Rath Packing Company gained a reputation for high-quality meats and had become a major supplier in the mid-continent market. In the mid-1940s, the company built in its headquarters city of Waterloo, Iowa, a multimillion-dollar plant, which then was the most modern in the industry. At that time, Rath's total employment was over eight thousand. By the late 1970s, when the employee ownership issue arose, the company had been going downhill almost steadily for three decades. Earlier in the 1970s, the union had agreed to financial sacrifices in order to help the company to survive. In the financial crisis of 1978 and 1979, the union was faced with management demands for even more drastic sacrifices. After considerable internal discussion, the leaders responded that they were unwilling to negotiate any further sacrifices unless these were exchanged for employee ownership. The board of directors decided that, indeed, some sort of shift to employee ownership presented the only possibility for saving the company.

Over a period of months, the union bargaining committee, led by Local 46 president Lyle Taylor and chief steward Charles Mueller, negotiated with management to arrive at the following plan: the substantial sacrifices in fringe benefits the workers were making would be channeled into an escrow bank account that would be turned over to the company only when the transfer of ownership had been completed. In other words, workers agreed to save the

company $5 million in labor costs, with that savings being chan-
neled into the strengthening of the capital base of the company.
The parties agreed also that, upon the transfer of ownership,
workers would have $20 a week deducted from their pay for a
period of more than two years, and this money would be used to
provide the workers with 60 percent of Rath stock; 40 percent of
the stock would remain with private investors.' About seventy
members of management also committed themselves to this payroll
deduction.

The parties also agreed to profit sharing, 50 percent going to
the company and 50 percent to workers. But there would be no
sharing of profits until a substantial deficit in the pension fund had
been covered. Since the workers were primarily interested in saving their jobs in a desperate financial situation, they were not
concerned about whether this plan would ever yield them any
profits.

The indispensable final piece to the financial package was supplied by the U.S. Department of Housing and Urban Development
in the form of a $4.6 million Urban Development Action Grant.
The money was granted to the city of Waterloo, which passed it
through to the company as a loan. Several years earlier, before any
question of employee ownership arose, the Economic Development
Administration had carried out a similar project, granting $3 million
to the Black Hawk Economic Development Committee, a local
agency created by county government, which in turn loaned that
money to the Rath company. Without the EDA money, it would
have been impossible to keep Rath from bankruptcy until the conversion to employee ownership was worked out.

These two grant-loan projects made the Rath Packing Company an important asset to the city and county. Not only does
Rath continue to provide jobs and a continuing source of tax reve-
nues, but as long as Rath survives and is able to meet the payments
of principal and interest on the loans to county and city, local
officials in the Waterloo metropolitan area can count on a substantial flow of money to be used for economic development projects
that previously would have been beyond local financial capacities.

The employee take-over of the company was completed in

June 1980, after votes by majorities of both the workers and the existing private stockholders affirming the plan negotiated by management and the union. Under this plan, the preexisting board of directors of six members was expanded by ten new members nominated by the union. The plan also involved the establishment of an employee stock ownership trust to vote the shares owned by workers, including the shares still to be purchased for worker accounts until the goal of 60 percent of the stock had been reached. Under a novel plan, which appears to be the first of its kind, members of the board of trustees are elected by workers on the basis of one-worker-one-vote, and, by voting 60 percent of the stock, the trustees control the board of directors. In other words, the voting procedure is completely in conformity with the principles of a worker cooperative, and also with the principles and procedures followed in local union elections.

It was no easy task to work out such an innovative arrangement. The first plan agreed upon by the parties was not based upon existing ESOP legislation and was disapproved by the U.S. Department of Labor on the grounds that it was illegal to establish any employee benefit program that invested more than 10 percent of its funds in the securities of the employer. Union and company officials appealed to the department to reverse its decision, arguing that ERISA provisions should apply only to pension plans, and the employee stock ownership plan was not designed to supplant existing pension plans, which remained in force though underfunded. When the department remained firm in its original interpretation, the parties decided to establish an official employee stock ownership plan, since ESOP legislation allows for most or all of the funds invested in the plan to be in the form of stock of the employer. Because the union leaders were determined to work out a new type of ESOP that would provide maximum democratic safeguards to the voting rights of workers, the complex and unfamiliar problem in legal design (worked out by attorney Jack Curtis) substantially delayed the final approval of the Rath ESOP until December 1980, about six months after the change in ownership and control.

This delay presented the parties with serious problems. In order to secure worker acceptance of employee ownership, the union leaders had promised members that the shift in ownership would be accompanied by the appointment of a new chief executive officer in whom the union leaders and members would have confidence. During the spring of 1980, the union leaders had held serious discussions with two highly experienced meat-packing executives who were interested in assuming the CEO position. When they were at the point of asking a formal commitment from the man of their choice, they learned that he had been killed in an airplane crash. They then telephoned to seek a formal commitment from their second choice, only to hear that he had suddenly died. This extraordinarily bad luck left the union without a candidate for chief executive officer at the time when the parties had to go to press with materials to be distributed to the stockholders for their vote on the ownership change. Since these materials had to include the names of those nominated to be board members and the chief executive officer, the union had no choice but to approve the continuation in office of the incumbent.

The employee stock ownership plan that was finally worked out had to be approved by the stockholders, and the board of directors decided that it would be unwise to make a change of CEO until the plan was ratified. This meant that for the first months of the majority ownership by its employees, Rath continued without a change in top company leadership. A subcommittee of the board began a search for the new CEO in November 1980, but this was not an easy position to fill. The company needed not only a highly competent executive but one interested in working in a situation in which the workers, through their union, held ultimate control. Beyond the apparent risk of assuming the position with such an unprecedented ownership arrangement was the fact that it would take extraordinary efforts by management and workers to reestablish Rath as a viable company. This meant that any serious candidate would have to be one who found the job more interesting and challenging than conventional executive positions. In Herbert Epstein, a man in his mid-fifties who had already had a distinguished business career, the parties found such an individual. But it was not until May 1, 1981—more than ten months after the ownership change—that he was able to assume the new position.

The delay in appointing a new chief executive officer had a negative effect upon relations between union leaders and the rank and file. The union leaders had promised the members that the change to majority employee ownership would be accompanied by a change in top management. Even though the union leaders had valid explanations for the delay, these legal and procedural questions were beyond the experience of the rank and file, and some members were inclined to think that Taylor and Mueller had been bought off by the existing top management and had agreed not to press for the promised changes.

The delay in getting the employee stock ownership plan in place also raised doubts among some members regarding the good faith and competence of the union leaders. The members had been led to expect that the stock they were purchasing would be credited to their accounts as soon as payroll deductions began with the installation of the new board of directors in June 1980. At this point the payroll deductions did indeed begin, but the union leaders had to explain that papers confirming the amount and progress of their stock purchases would not be forthcoming until the ESOP was officially in place, which finally occurred six months later in December. These tensions between union leaders and the rank and file will probably continue to occur in other employee purchases as long as the complexities of the transition to employee ownership are little understood by union members and leaders. Leaders are likely to make in good faith promises that they are unable to keep, and then rank-and-filers may conclude that they have been deliberately misled.

THE UNION AND THE COMPOSITION OF THE BOARD

Trustees elected to hold the first positions on the employee stock ownership trust were nominated by the union leaders and ratified by the members. Since future annual elections of trustees will continue to be by vote among the members, there is ample opportunity for opponents of the existing leadership to choose an opposition slate and campaign for it.

In choosing the ten new board members to be formally elected by the trustees, the union leaders had to balance two considerations. They wanted people strongly committed to worker interests and highly responsive to the information and opinions given them by the union leaders. On the other hand, they recognized that packing the new board entirely with rank-and-file workers was not a practical option. This would deprive the workers of some of the legal, financial, and administrative expertise that they needed. Furthermore, a board majority made up of rank-and-file workers would not be ratified by the existing board, representing private stockholders, nor would such a board win the confidence of officials of HUD, from which the essential government money was to come.

There was also serious discussion within the union as to whether president Lyle Taylor and chief steward Charles Mueller should be elected to the board. At the time the original decisions on board membership were made, Taylor and Mueller preferred to maintain a complete structural separation between union and management and therefore declined to take the board positions, although it was in their power to demand positions.

Of the ten new board members, three rank-and-file activists were selected from among workers by the union leaders. The other seven were all people who had attained some prominence in professional, business, or political affairs. For expertise and experience in management, the union selected a former Rath manufacturing executive, J. Sidney Oberman, and a Nebraska construction company executive, Leonard E. Dodson (uncle by marriage to Lyle Taylor). In the field of politics and community relations, the union chose former U.S. senator Richard C. Clark and former Iowa lieutenant governor Robert D. Fulton (brother-in-law of Chuck Mueller). Recognizing the need to improve race relations in the company, the union chose Walter L. Cunningham, a black high school principal noted both for his insistence on high academic standards and for his good relations with students, teachers, and parents. For expertise and experience in union affairs, the union chose Ralph Helstein, formerly president of the United Packing House Workers and then a member of the AFL-CIO executive board (Local 46 had belonged to this union before it was merged into the Amalgamated Meat Cutters and Butcher Workmen of North America).

Tove Hammer's position on the board resulted from her previous industrial relations and employee ownership research. When she and Robert Stern visited Waterloo at the request of the union leaders in May 1979, they spent two hours with the negotiating committee reviewing Cornell's research findings regarding different forms of employee ownership and the potentials and problems of each form. It was this discussion that led the negotiating committee to decide that, contrary to the legal advice they had previously received, to consolidate worker voting power, they would insist upon a plan that included a stock ownership trust, with the trustees being elected on as democratic a basis as possible.

When the position was offered her, Hammer replied that, while she was fully in sympathy with workers' aims in saving their jobs and maintaining a strong union and would as a board member welcome information and suggestions from union leaders, a position on the board involved a fiduciary responsibility to safeguard the interests of the company as a whole; and she would have to exercise her independent judgment on how those interests could best be served. The union leaders accepted her on those terms. We assume that similar conversations took place between the union leaders and other worker nominees for the board of directors. In other words, the union leaders secured new board members sympathetic to workers and to the union and committed to take seriously the ideas and opinions of the union leaders, but not committed to vote in accordance with union dictates.

This process of selection led to important consequences in the dynamics within the board and between the worker-elected board members and the union leaders. With ten worker-elected board members to six members who had represented private stockholders, one might assume that control of the board would immediately shift to the new majority. One might also expect that issues would now be thrashed out between the two factions, with decisions being made on a ten-to-six vote. But this was not the case. Charles Swisher, a highly respected Waterloo attorney, had chaired the board at the time of the negotiations leading to employee ownership. His leadership had been indispensable to the successful conclusion of the ownership shift. The union leaders trusted Swisher and were not pushing to show their power by insisting upon election of a new board chairperson. In this period, all board members were striving to save the company from bankruptcy, and this overarching concern tended to subordinate differences among members of the board. Leadership of the board, therefore, did not become an issue, and Swisher continued in that position.

In many companies, the board of directors performs primarily symbolic functions, simply ratifying the proposals of top management except in crisis situations. Such boards are not likely to meet more often than quarterly. From the beginning, the reconstituted Rath board has held monthly meetings. This cost the company a good deal in travel and living expenses for board members coming from out of town for meetings of the board and of subcommittees working on such critical matters as the search for a new chief executive officer. But a board that must oversee a thorough restructuring of management and of worker-management and union-management relations can hardly discharge these responsibilities with less frequent meetings; and the parties assume that as the new pattern develops, the frequency of board meetings can be substantially reduced.

So as to be fully informed on the views of the union leaders, Hammer and Helstein have made it a practice to come to Waterloo on the afternoon before board meetings for several hours of discussion with Taylor and Mueller. Other newly elected members of the board have joined these meetings when possible.

These pre–board meeting discussions were not simply briefing sessions. They involved very active consideration and at times— when the union leaders believed that the members they had selected were not pushing the union point of view strongly enough—sharp disagreements. Even though the parties had agreed in advance upon the role and responsibilities of the worker-elected directors, there remained conflicting interpretations of this role. For example, at one time when the arguments had been most heated, Mueller responded to Whyte's question about whether the union had expected its elected board members to be rubber stamps by saying, "No, but we knew what we wanted, and we expected them to help us get what we wanted." But some of the new board members believed that at times what the union leaders wanted for the members would not be in the best interest of the company or even in the best long-run interest of the workers, and they therefore had to retain the responsibility of exercising independent judgment.

Relations between the union leaders and the board members they had selected were complicated by two other factors. First, having been accustomed to an adversarial relationship with management and also to the resolution of differences within the union on the basis of majority voting, the union leaders expected issues that came before the board of directors to be decided in the same style of confrontation and voting. They found it hard to understand that on most issues the board was reaching a consensus and that, in fact, voting rarely took place. Second, there was a problem in transmitting accurately to the board union information and ideas when the union leaders did not sit on the board. Because the worker members played a rather passive role, the union leaders looked to the members they selected from outside the company to present their information and ideas. The outside board members were necessarily at a disadvantage in discussions with such members of top management as the controller and the chief executive officer who had much more detailed knowledge of operations. On some occasions, information received from union leaders has led an outside board member to make statements on a complex matter that in fact misinterpreted the information, and the outside member had to be corrected by management. This put the outside board member and the union leaders in awkward positions. Such difficulties in communication led in July 1981 to the board's decision to invite Lyle Taylor to assume membership on the board and to his decision to accept this offer. Since then, Taylor has had an opportunity to present union information and ideas directly to the board. Furthermore, since he had the respect of board members, he could be sure that he would get serious consideration for any information or ideas he presented, although he would have no assurance that his views would prevail. This shift in union and board positions was worked out with the full support of the new chief executive officer, Herbert Epstein.

The conversion to employee ownership required changes in the internal administration of the union as well as in its relations with management. The union leaders were determined to maintain the union structure and procedures regarding handling of grievances and other disputes with management. Guidance of these activities fell to Chief Steward Mueller while President Taylor became more concerned with matters affecting the top management of the company. In other situations, this division of labor might provoke a serious split between the two top local union leaders, but Taylor and Mueller were close friends and had worked together for many years. So far, this has helped them to resolve whatever differences have arisen.

COOPERATIVE PROBLEM SOLVING AND PRODUCTIVITY

The shift to employee ownership has involved a major change in worker-management relations, from the shop floor to the highest levels. The union leaders recognized that change in ownership and a major infusion of new capital would not be sufficient to restore to economic health a company that was sliding into bankruptcy. Only if union and management could cooperate on a comprehensive program to improve productivity and the quality of working life would it be possible to assure the survival of the company. The financial situation was so critical that the parties could not afford to wait for the change in ownership to be consummated before starting the cooperative program.

In the fall of 1979 Chris Meek and Warner Woodworth visited Waterloo to discuss with the union leaders the development of such a program. As research associate with Cornell University's Program on New Systems of Work and Participation, Meek had had three-and-a-half years of experience with the Jamestown Area Labor-Management Committee. Woodworth, a professor of organizational behavior at Brigham Young University, had consulted with the Muskegon, Michigan, Labor-Management Committee and had had extensive experience in organizational development in private industry. In December 1979, Whyte joined Meek and Woodworth in Waterloo to talk further with the union leaders and to propose to management the establishment of the kind of cooperative problem-solving program that had been developed in Jamestown.

The parties established a top-level steering committee jointly chaired by union and management officials to meet monthly and plan activities and monitor developments. Some months later, the parties also agreed to the establishment of a strategic planning group so that union leaders could participate with management in studying and working out plans for the future of the company. The next step was the establishment of action research teams in some of the major departments. These teams followed the Jamestown procedures, beginning with a wide-ranging discussion of problems facing a given department and then moving to establish priorities. As problems arose that needed more detailed attention, the action research teams established miniteams or assigned individuals to gather information and develop ideas for action.

In all these activities, workers not only voiced complaints and suggestions but were actively involved in working out solutions. No problems were declared out of bounds. For example, the program to revive the company involved major investments in new machines. Salespeople, who were accustomed to meeting with executives in top management offices, were surprised to find themselves talking also with rank-and-file workers in the departments where the new machines were to be installed. The workers did not hold back from raising questions and expressing opinions based on their long years of experience in production and processing operations. These discussions were educational for all parties. At times, the salespeople found workers' questions more difficult to answer than management questions, and the management people came to recognize that workers were alerting them to problems that would inevitably arise in the installation and operation of the machines.

Beginning in February 1981, Cornell graduate student Kate Squire moved to Waterloo to become a participant observer in the cooperative problem-solving process. Since Meek and Woodworth were only able to spend two to three days a month in Waterloo, Squire's presence made it possible to establish more continuity to the program. Under the general guidance of Meek and Woodworth, and in consultation with Whyte, she participated in the start up of a number of action research teams, sat in on team meetings and sought to facilitate the process of problem definition and problem solving.

CEO Herbert Epstein sought from the beginning to develop a close working relationship with the union leaders. At the same time, he faced a difficult set of problems within management. With the shift in power to the union, middle managers and foremen were generally insecure and uncertain about what powers remained in their hands. Union leaders believed that some strategic changes needed to be made in management personnel in order to support the cooperative program, but at the outset Epstein felt it necessary to assure his management people that he would make no precipitous personnel decisions and seek to give them the support they needed. Some such assurance was probably necessary since there had been some occasions in which workers had threatened to have a foreman fired, claiming that the union now had this power. After the first few months as CEO, Epstein made a series of strategic personnel changes designed both to strengthen management and to provide further support to the cooperative program.

During his first week as Rath CEO, Epstein had held an open house reception to which all Rath employees were invited. This unprecedented occasion was important in symbolizing the new worker-management relationship, but he needed several months of day-to-day involvement in order to give substance to the new symbolism. In late August 1981, Epstein, in collaboration with the union leaders, conducted a large public meeting to which family members as well as employees were invited. The meeting was designed to present a state-of-the-company report and to propose goals whose attainment was necessary to secure the survival of Rath. According to the comments of workers, those attending were favorably impressed with the openness of management in laying out in full detail the critical financial situation of the company, and they responded well to Epstein's expressions of appreciation for worker and union cooperation in securing the gains already achieved.

Epstein proposed a goal of a further 20 percent productivity improvement during the next year as essential for the company's survival. Such an ambitious goal can have meaning for employees only if it is translated into subgoals for each department and then backed up by a social process designed to turn goals into achievements. Epstein followed up the large public meeting with meetings in each department. These provided opportunities for discussion with workers and union leaders about the problems and potentials of effecting the needed improvements.

The HUD grant-loan made possible major investments in technological modernization. These changes were carried out with the active participation of workers and union leaders. But since the major gains in productivity achieved in several departments must be credited partly to the new machines, it is impossible to measure the contributions of human factors.

One of the earliest successes was achieved in the sliced bacon department where action research teams worked out plans for new production lines. The increase in productivity was estimated at approximately 20 percent. Action research teams in the abattoir have worked on problems of productivity, safety, and quality of working life in the hog kill department and in the cut department. Management estimates productivity gains in the abattoir at $950,000 for a thirty-nine-week period ending June 1, 1981.

Management and union leaders recognized serious inefficiencies in the maintenance department, which were compounded by poor communication between maintenance and the production departments it serves. Action research teams on both shifts, including representatives of each craft and supervisors, have been working intensively on improving both communications between shifts and with production and the system of allocating work and managing parts and supplies.

One of the most important gains is also the most difficult to measure: the improvement in the quality of human resources through worker, manager, and supervisor involvement in the joint problem-solving process. Perhaps the most dramatic examples in this field are worker volunteers who, inspired by their participation in action research teams, have been seeking opportunities for training so that they can improve their problem-solving skills and increase their value to themselves as well as to the company. Most of the work of the action research teams has been done on volunteered time, with workers coming in half an hour before their shift for meetings and pursuing individual assignments after the shift. When approximately twenty-five workers expressed an interest in learning more about group problem solving, Meek, Woodworth, and Squire developed a training program. The Federal Mediation and Conciliation Service also contributed to the training process with courses for stewards and foremen.

Can Rath be considered a success story? If success is interpreted in terms of achieving long-term economic viability, it is clear that Rath is far from reaching this goal. But the struggle for survival at Rath must be seen in the context of a depressed meat-packing industry and a severe economic recession during which the media often report cases of plant shutdowns and even of companies going out of business. Anyone familiar with the Rath case recognizes that only the shift to employee ownership and worker participation has made it possible for the company to survive for two years beyond the ownership change and to win a fighting chance for long-term survival. In the meantime, Rath has maintained jobs and a tax base particularly important to the severely depressed city of Waterloo.

The story of Rath Packing Company has also evoked wide popular and media interest throughout the country. The influence of its example has grown as the principal actors in that case have become prominent members of the rapidly growing networks of workers, union and management leaders, and academicians interested in employee ownership. This is manifest not only in their participation in conferences around the country but more importantly in the information and advice they are asked to give to people considering employee ownership to save jobs. Warner Woodworth took what he learned in his action research role at Rath to assist in the establishment of Hyatt Clark Industries. The experience Jack Curtis gained in working out the ESOP at Rath helped him in guiding the union leaders of Pan Am Multiunion Labor Council in working out their ESOP. It is no coincidence that the Philadelphia area employees of A&P belong to the same union that represents Rath workers. Besides playing leading roles in meetings and conferences on employee ownership, Lyle Taylor and Herbert Epstein are frequently called upon for information and advice. While no one associated with Rath claims to have *the* answer on saving jobs with employee ownership, there is a growing public recognition of the importance of learning from experience at Rath, the first case in which the union led the campaign to save jobs through employee ownership and labor-management cooperative problem solving.

HYATT CLARK INDUSTRIES

The Hyatt Clark Industries case parallels the Rath case in some respects but differs in others. Again, it was local union leaders who organized the job-saving campaign, and they too were determined to secure worker rights both in ownership and in participation in management. But this was not a case of an entire firm going out of business. The plant in Clark, New Jersey, belonged to General Motors, which meant that the establishment of employee ownership involved negotiations between the local leaders at Clark and the management of one of the nation's most important companies. Although agreement was reached only after long and difficult negotiations, it is important to note that agreement would have been impossible if General Motors had adhered to the uncooperative management policies that were typical of the 1970s cases (Sokoloff 1982).

General Motors announced on August 8, 1980, its intention to close the Clark plant within six months. When the parties were still engaged in serious negotiations as this deadline approached, General Motors made the essential commitment to keep the plant operating as negotiations continued. Final agreement was reached only in October 1981, fourteen months after the shutdown announcement.

The decision to close the plant appears to have been motivated by several factors. The Clark plant manufactured ball bearings for rear-wheel drive cars, and General Motors was shifting the bulk of its production to front-wheel drive vehicles. The Clark plant had been losing money for several years. It was the locus of continuing labor relations problems between General Motors and the local union and between the UAW local and the international officers; some Clark people believed that in preparation for the next national negotiations General Motors wished to use this case to impress UAW top leadership with the need to make wage concessions, which naturally worried UAW's regional and national officials.

General Motors officials, however, recognized certain advantages to keeping the Clark plant open as an employee-owned company. General Motors was not abandoning rear-wheel drive cars altogether and thus could continue to use the Clark plant as a source for bearings. Also, a shutdown in the same area where the giant Ford Mahwah assembly plant had been shut down would have resulted in severe social and economic problems for thousands of workers, their families, and their communities. It is difficult to weigh the force of the social responsibility question with General Motors management, but this does seem to have added impetus to management's desire to avoid the public relations costs of another major automotive shutdown.

Local UAW leaders James May and James Zarrello took the lead in pushing the idea of a worker buy-out with their members. To raise money for a feasibility study, they proposed a payroll deduction to increase union dues for several months. They were stunned when the membership voted this down by a narrow margin. Several factors seem to have been involved in this negative vote. Leaders of a strong local opposition faction argued that, if the union just stood firm and refused to consider changes, General Motors would back down and decide the company could not get along without the Clark plant. Furthermore, many of the workers had long years of service with GM and would be entitled to substantial pensions if their early retirement was caused by a shutdown. Because relations were strained between the local and the UAW regional office, the regional officials made no effort to intervene to encourage a favorable vote.

Just when the union local vote had seemed to kill the project, key members of local management decided to cast their lot with the Clark plant and proposed a joint union-management employee ownership committee. The union leaders accepted this plan and worked with management to raise money for the feasibility study through voluntary contributions. Everyone who wished to work for the employee-owned company was required to pledge $100. More than half those on the payroll signed up, pledging $120,000.

The new plan appears to have been more attractive to employees than the first union proposal for two reasons. With key members of local management backing employee ownership, the project no longer seemed just a pipe dream in the minds of a small group of workers. Furthermore, voluntary contributions left those seeking early retirement out of the decision-making process.

The feasibility study carried out by Arthur D. Little and Company indicated a good possibility of economic viability for a new company employing about half those currently on the payroll (or on temporary layoff), providing the union would agree to a 25 percent pay reduction and General Motors would contract to buy a major portion of the plant's output for a three-year transitional period.

There followed a long and complicated negotiation process between General Motors and the Clark joint committee and between management and the union within the plant. A key figure in these negotiations was Alan V. Lowenstein, a New Jersey attorney who had played a major role with the New Jersey Job Development Authority and EDA in the employee buy-out of Okonite Company. During these negotiations, the local union leaders consulted frequently with Warner Woodworth, drawing on the expertise he had gained working with labor and management at Rath Packing Company.

In Lowenstein's view, to assure the potential sources of financing and key members of management of the economic viability of the firm, it would be necessary to grant management full control of the firm at least in the early years of its existence. The union leaders reluctantly agreed to a plan whereby worker-owned stock would not be voted until it was fully vested (paid for), ten years after the creation of the new firm. The union also accepted Lowenstein's proposal on the constitution of the board of directors: three selected by the union, three by management, and seven prominent outsiders selected, in effect, by Lowenstein. Thus, as interpreted by the union leaders themselves, management through Lowenstein has firm control of the company through its first decade. The three union-selected board members are local leaders James May and James Zarrello and Warner Woodworth.

Negotiations between local union and local management nearly broke down on the question of distribution of stock. Management first insisted that stock be distributed in relation to salary levels, as is usually done with ESOPs. The union insisted on equal distribution regardless of salary. At first some management people regarded the union's position as "ridiculous" (Sokoloff 1982), but the union leaders argued that worker jobs were at stake as much as management jobs, and their demand finally prevailed. The agreement, however, did not call for an employee stock ownership trust designed to consolidate worker voting power.

Since the feasibility study indicated that a 25 percent pay cut was necessary for success of the new company, this cut, which still left Clark workers above prevailing wage rates in the area, was accepted without serious argument by the union. The agreement did, however, provide for profit sharing as well as for worker stock ownership.

The most difficult issue between the Clark joint committee and General Motors was the company's responsibility for pension and early retirement benefits for its former employees. The joint committee was adamant in seeking to maintain these benefits, and General Motors was concerned with a potential liability that might be as high as $60 million. The issue was resolved when the parties agreed that one quarter of this potential sum, $15 million, would be added to the purchase price.

General Motors agreed to take $10 million in nonvoting stock, thus reducing the price by that amount. The corporation also provided $15 million in interim financing until the loan from Prudential Insurance Company was approved. While loan arrangements were worked out with Chemical Bank, the company also provided bridge financing, taking as collateral pledges of common stock and promissory notes for inventories. Finally, General Motors signed a contract, based on its estimate of sales of cars requiring the type of bearing made at the Clark plant to take up to 80 percent of the plant's output for the first three years. This meant the output of a work force cut about in half, and unfortunately General Motors was not able to meet the provisional goal of purchases during the early months of the agreement because of the drastic decline in its car sales.

While the agreement on voting rights and board membership places management firmly in control for the present, management did agree with the union to develop an active program of worker participation. Warner Woodworth has assumed responsibility for guiding this program, working particularly with top management. Wynn Hausser of Cornell University and Mary DelaMare of Brigham Young University have been conducting intensive training sessions, developing a participatory system for worker representatives and supervisors.

OTHER SIGNIFICANT CASES

Employee ownership is emerging as a major strategy to maintain jobs in food retailing and to maintain efficient food marketing services within cities. For some years, the Great Atlantic and Pacific Tea Company (A&P) has been closing stores throughout the country in response to continuing financial losses. According to James Wood, chairman of A&P, the company is giving up on seventy stores in the Philadelphia area "as a lost cause" (*New York Times*, May 23, 1982). The employees in the Philadelphia area are represented by Local 1357 of the United Food and Commercial Workers, the same union which represents Rath workers. Led by President Wendell Young of Local 1357, the union has reached an agreement with A&P that is designed to reopen many if not all of the company's closed stores in the area under the name of Super Fresh Food Centers. At this writing, the twenty-three stores have been reopened, with union members getting preference in rehiring.

Under the new contract, the workers are to be cut from $10 an hour to $8, with the possibility of recovering the old rate within two years. They are also cutting Sunday overtime pay from double time to time and a half. The *New York Times* reported on May 23, 1982,

> In the critical clause of the agreement, the company will set aside earnings equivalent to 1 percent of gross sales in the reopened stores for its employees. Of that, 40 percent will be distributed in incentive bonuses and the rest will be held in a fund toward the purchase of stores. The union has the right of first refusal for all the closed stores before they are sold to outsiders.
>
> The food union has exercised an option on two of the shuttered markets and are now seeking financing to complete the purchase, Mr. Young said. The down payments will come from a fund of $3 million gathered in pledges from union members.
>
> A&P's competitors in the area are taking a close look at the ground-breaking pact.
>
> Mr. Young said that other chains had been in touch with him but had said that because the agreement was so experimental "you can't put a price tag on it for another year."
>
> Michael Rourke, vice president for marketing for A&P, said the chain looked at the unusual labor agreement as "an experiment" and had no immediate plans to apply it on a large scale. "We'll see how it develops," he said. "We're very optimistic about it."

In the early stages of these negotiations, union leaders sought advice and information from Cornell University, and they are now working closely with consultants from the Wharton School of the University of Pennsylvania and from the St. Joseph's College Food Marketing Institute.

This case has significance far beyond the interests of the company, the union, and workers and members of their families. Closing supermarkets, especially in central cities, has been an accelerating trend in recent years. Food chains have shifted their resources to middle-class city areas and to suburban markets. This leaves millions of poor people in city slums stranded, having to fall back on small mom-and-pop stores, thus reinforcing the inequitable situation in which, as various commentators have noted, the poor pay more. If the A&P–UFCWU experiment is successful, employee ownership can become an important force in the redevelopment of the economies of the central cities.

In March 1982, National Steel announced its intention to close its subsidiary, Weirton Steel Company in Weirton, West Virginia, and at the same time offered employees the opportunity to buy the company. According to National Steel, Weirton had not been losing money, but the previous year earned less than 1 percent on its investment. According to all accounts, most of the equipment and facilities are quite modern, unlike the case of Youngstown Sheet and Tube Company, which had been so neglected by its conglomerate owner that astronomical sums would have been required at the outset to restore its competitive position. A study conducted by McKinsey and Company and released in late July 1982 indicated that an employee-owned Weirton Steel Company would be feasible, providing the workers agreed to a 20 percent cut in wage and benefit costs with an additional 12 percent wage and benefit deferral for a maximum of four years. McKinsey also recommended that the current level of employment of 8,200 be reduced to 7,000 over a ten-year period and that reinvestments of a maximum of $1.1 billion be made over the same period. This indicates that the approximately 3,300 workers currently on layoff have little chance of being reemployed in the Weirton steel mills. Weirton pay and benefit costs are estimated to be about two dollars above the average for workers covered by the national United Steelworkers contract; the proposed concessions would bring them well below the national agreement rates but would still leave Weirton workers in a good position in relation to average rates in manufacturing industry in general.

The transfer of ownership depends not only on these concessions but also on the price for the mills established in negotiations with National Steel and agreement on responsibility for the currently underfunded pension liabilities, which proved to be a major problem in negotiating the sale of Hyatt Clark Industries.

While the Independent Steel Workers Union at Weirton is cooperating with management on the employee ownership project, it remains to be seen to what extent a union that has been dominated by the company can break out of the paternalistic relationship and become a worker-controlled force for a democratically managed, employee-owned company.

Since Weirton Steel dominates the local economy of the city of Weirton and its surrounding area and is the second largest taxpayer in the state of West Virginia, this case is of great importance to state and local government officials, who are seeking to help work out the ownership transfer.

We are also finding minority ownership programs initiated by unions. When Pan American World Airways called upon its unions to take a 10 percent wage cut to save the company from bankruptcy, the leaders of a multiunion employee labor council bargained to get $1 in stock for every $3 they gave up in wages. They also received a commitment to put union representatives on the board of directors. Richard Phenneger, a leader of the labor council, estimates that the agreement will eventually give employees between 12 and 16 percent of Pan American stock (Rosen 1982). If worker stock is voted in a bloc, as council members intend, this could pose a serious threat to management control in the case of a proxy battle. The labor council and the management have also agreed to work together in developing a companywide worker participation program.

EMPLOYEE OWNERSHIP AND THE FUTURE OF COLLECTIVE BARGAINING

The 1980 cases of union leadership in shaping employee ownership, from Rath to Hyatt Clark to A&P to Pan American, make evident that there is an important change occurring in industrial

relations. The fears—or hopes—of some that transfers of ownership to employees would lead them to abandon their unions have
not been justified by experience. Unions remain in place, but to
what extent is employee ownership changing collective bargaining?
It is too early to tell. The problem is not only the short span of
experience but also the fact that these shifts in ownership are occurring during a recession period when concession bargaining has
become the order of the day in many sectors of private industry.
This makes it impossible to disentangle the effects of the ownership
shift from the effects of the recession.

Given these limitations, we offer, based on the cases we have
studied so far, the following highly speculative predictions:

1. Union leaders in employee-owned firms will strive to
keep as close as possible to the pattern of contracts bargained
in the private sector of their industry. In the case of a private
company in financial distress, the union leaders will agree to
undercut that national pattern only if such concessions are
clearly necessary in order to prevent plant shutdowns.

2. The unions will remain active in handling grievances of
individuals and groups of workers. In a large company, even
worker representation on the board of directors will not obvi-
ate the need for union representation on shop-level problems.

3. While the bargaining and grievance processes will remain
somewhat adversarial, increasingly unions will cooperate with
management in problem solving designed to improve productivity and the quality of work life. However, this does not
mean that union leaders will simply follow management in this
field. Increasingly unions will demand that such programs be
jointly planned and administered. In other words, unions will
negotiate the terms under which the cooperative program will
be implemented.

Employee ownership has major consequences not only for
union and management leaders but also for public officials responsible for regional economic development. The leaders in these various sectors of society now face the challenge of rethinking their
policies in response to the changes taking place.

6.
Policy Options
for Unions, Management,
and Goverment

William Foote Whyte

WHILE LABOR-MANAGEMENT cooperation and employee ownership may not provide *the* means for economic revitalization of America, they show enough promise to be included in any public policy agenda for our nation. This final chapter considers how unions, management, and government can best strengthen the employment potentials found in cooperative problem solving and employee ownership.

EMPLOYEE PARTICIPATION:
IMPLICATIONS FOR MANAGEMENT AND UNIONS

The current surge of interest in employee participation will be constructive only if management thinking advances beyond the gimmick stage. Unless management recognizes that the company is a social system made up of mutually dependent parts and that the introduction of change at low levels in the organization must be supported by changes in other parts of the system, worker participation will come to be seen as a foreign element, which is bound to be ejected from the company. This does not mean that management must totally change its style before introducing worker participation but that success in the development of participation in the shop depends upon a process of building participation throughout the organization. If this process is not instituted, worker participation is bound to be just another fad, to be abandoned when the next fad comes along.

If unions are to play important roles in the development of worker participation programs, then a major reorientation is required of union leaders also. Until recently, most international officers viewed worker participation programs with deep suspicion, if not with outright hostility. They believed that such programs were simply management devices to win worker loyalty away from unions and to distract worker attention from the basic issues of wages, hours, and working conditions. Their suspicions were reinforced by cases of company officials who talked of cooperation regarding a unionized plant but fought union organizing drives elsewhere and by industrial leaders who supported right-to-work laws and lobbied against labor reform legislation backed by the AFL-CIO. This mistrust is certainly not without foundation. Many executives may indeed see quality of working life and other participation programs as means of winning worker loyalty away from unions. This attitude, however, does not automatically prescribe what policies the union should adopt in response to management initiatives in this field.

If management proposes to start a program purportedly designed to improve the quality of working life, can the union afford to stand idly by or risk opposing something that might prove popular with many workers? A labor leader who was advocating worker participation long before the idea became popular with management, Irving Bluestone, former UAW vice president, gives this answer:

> Within the UAW at one point, when GM was engaged in its southern strategy and was using the teamwork group to satisfy workers and keep them from voting for the union, this issue was sharply drawn on the international executive board. One of the members of the board said, "They're using this as an anti-union device! How can you support it? What you have to do is tell the corporation to cut it out!" I

sad, "That's fine: You want me to say to Tom Murphy, 'Treat the workers like dogs—don't treat them nicely,' so that the union would be advocating that workers be oppressed and exploited, so that we'd be able to organize them! I'm not about to do that!'"

Bluestone sees an essential role for unions in quality of working life and similar programs:

> I am convinced that, despite initial successes with programs which are designed, planned, and implemented solely by management, management will eventually abuse it and people will become unhappy. As one of the Ford management people put it to me recently: if you leave it up to management alone, they'll find a way to screw it up.

Furthermore, Bluestone believes that "a union's role is to take the lead, and to come up with ideas, and not wait for management to do something." He places his own ideas in philosophical context:

> The notion of unionism is to bring into the workplace not only decent standards in the economic life of the workman and his family, and decent working conditions, but to bring some measure of democratic values into the workplace. . . .
>
> If a worker as an adult is a free citizen in a free society, why then should he be deprived of all these rights when he becomes a worker in the workplace? (Simmons 1982).

What appeared until recently to be simply the vision of an impractical dreamer is now taking concrete form in such leading companies as General Motors, Ford Motor Company, Xerox, and an increasing number of other firms. The central feature of these programs is that they are jointly designed and implemented by management and union leaders. Similarly, area labor-management committees, like the one in Jamestown, are governed jointly by leaders of labor and management. When unions participate as equal partners in these programs, they can not only avoid the risk of having workers manipulated against union interests but also win increasing union loyalty as they serve members in new ways.

The union's decision to work with management in cooperative problem solving answers one policy question, but it leaves unresolved the nature of the relationship between labor-management committees and collective bargaining. As argued in chapter 3, it is unrealistic to assume that the two sets of union-management activities can be kept completely separate. If labor-management committees are to go beyond cosmetic changes, their activities will inevitably lead them into terrain that has been traditionally reserved for collective bargaining. It is too early to say how these two areas of activity may best be related to each other. All that can be said now is that, if union-management cooperative problem solving is to yield its potential benefits, the parties need to be concerned with developing a new pattern of collective bargaining.

EMPLOYEE OWNERSHIP: IMPLICATIONS FOR UNION POLICIES

Two factors seem to have been particularly influential in building the more favorable attitudes of high-level union leaders toward employee ownership. First, union leaders have noted the increasing use of employee ownership to prevent plant shutdowns, with favorable consequences for both workers and unions. In monitoring this trend, we have encountered only one case in which workers voted to decertify their union after the buy-out. In that case, Jeanette Glass, local union leaders claim they took this step after leaders of their international had flatly refused to give them any help in the buy-out; sometime later, the workers apparently decided they needed an organization after all and formed an independent union. Furthermore, Joseph Blasi reports in a personal communication two cases in which workers joined a union *after* the establishment of an employee stock ownership plan.

The second factor appears to be the unions' loss of faith in the ability of management to maintain profitable and productive enterprises. Until recently, union leaders have been inclined to believe that management people had the talents and the will necessary to assure the financial strength and productive efficiency of the enterprises, and that union leaders could best serve their members by concentrating on extracting from management as much of company income as they could gain through bargaining. In this age of conglomeration, that faith has been destroyed. Union leaders are recognizing that chief executives of many of our leading companies are concentrating on buying and selling companies or avoiding being taken over by other companies. In pursuit of that bottom line, executives are shutting down plants that are profitable, if only marginally so, and shifting their investments abroad. If management can no longer be trusted to maintain jobs, union leaders then naturally seek to give unions a more active role in job creation and preservation. Employee ownership provides a new and increasingly attractive alternative.

This shift in leadership thinking can best be illustrated by a recent statement by James Smith, assistant to the president of the United Steelworkers of America. After discussing some of the pitfalls of employee ownership, he went on to state,

> I certainly wouldn't fear for the future of the U.S.W.A. if every employer in the United States became an ESOP company.
>
> However, there are some minimal conditions of ESOPs that unions will demand, I believe. These include the following:
>
> (1) That employee stock ownership only occur *in addition* to an adequate, funded pension plan. In other words, if employees buy stock they should do so out of current earnings while they are active workers, rather than as a substitute for insured retirement income.
>
> (2) That full pass-through of voting rights be made to every employee on an equitable basis, with no subterfuge or managerial manipulation such as occurred at South Bend Lathe or most other small ESOPs.
>
> (3) That the stock issued to employees also be marketed publicly, so that there can be some outside judgment of its worth as an investment. In cases where this is impossible there should be a periodic outside appraisal by a firm jointly picked by representatives of workers and managers (Smith 1982).

This statement is of great significance both because the Steelworkers are such an important union and also because their experience with South Bend Lathe earlier had provoked strong opposition to employee stock ownership.

Note, however, the conditional acceptance of ESOPs. What should an international officer do when faced with a management demand that the pension plan be sacrificed in order to establish the ESOP? Is it in the best interests of the union itself to reject such a proposal out of hand? In a case such as South Bend Lathe, if workers are convinced that giving up their pension plan is necessary to save the jobs, the local union can agree to such a settlement in violation of orders from the central office.

Perhaps international officers should consider a different strategy. They might insist that the sacrifice of the pension plan be accepted only as a last resort and when all other options have been thoroughly explored and evaluated. They can propose that union and management make a joint study of labor and other costs and of productivity in the hope of discovering ways of meeting the financial problems of an employee-owned company without sacrificing the pension plan. Even if this joint study indicates poor prospects for company survival if the pension plan is maintained without changes, the union does not have to treat this matter as an all-or-nothing question. The union can negotiate some reductions in the cost and benefits of the pension plan, seeking particularly to ensure protection for workers with longer service.

Employee ownership, even when limited to a minority interest, can provide union leaders with a powerful weapon in bargaining with a financially distressed company. In the past, when management claimed that a wage cut was necessary to assure the survival of the company, union leaders were faced with two painful alternatives. They could assume that management was bluffing and therefore refuse to negotiate the pay cut—thus increasing the risk that the company actually would go out of business—or they could accept a financial sacrifice, getting nothing in return. Now when management claims a pay cut is necessary for the survival of the company, it is increasingly likely that the Pan Am scenario will be played out:

Management makes its demand.

Union leaders reply that, if management can persuade them of the gravity of the company's financial condition, they are willing to negotiate a pay cut, but they want to know how much stock workers will receive in return.

If management is willing to negotiate on these terms, the union leaders ask how many positions on the board of directors should go with how much stock.

This trend promises to impose new responsibilities on international union leaders and staff people advising local unions. No longer will they be able to consider the value of stock and forms of stock ownership irrelevant to workers and the local union leaders.

They will have to prepare themselves to provide solid information and advice to local union leaders who are considering employee stock ownership plans. While this greatly amplifies the scope of responsibilities for international officers, changes of much the same magnitude have taken place in the past. It has always been much simpler for unions to bargain in terms of hourly rates of pay, but decades ago union leaders recognized, beginning with the garment industry, that management control of piece rates could drastically affect the earnings of workers. In order to deal effectively with the industrial engineers and time study people, unions found it necessary to hire and train their own specialists in the analysis of the technical aspects of setting and changing piece rates.

Until recent months, leaders of international unions have met each plant shutdown and potential employee ownership case on an ad hoc basis, without having any preestablished plans or policies. This has led to conflict between the international officials and local union leaders, who charge that they have been getting no help from the international in saving jobs. If only to preserve the strength of the international union, top officers will have to develop policies, plans, and staff capabilities to deal with employee ownership.

In a field where substantial technical and financial expertise is required, few international unions will be able to provide staff to meet all membership needs regarding employee ownership. Each international might, however, develop a small staff that monitors trends in this field, is familiar with research findings, and can recommend to local unions consultants who are both knowledgeable and trustworthy. Furthermore, some union leaders might consider following the lead of the United Food and Commercial Workers Union in its unique contract with A&P. The creation of the investment fund, which is estimated to bring in $1.5 million a year, provides a resource base not only for financing worker-owned firms but also for developing the union's own technical assistance staff and for contracting with outside specialists.

If it is clearly impractical to maintain employment through continuing to make the products produced under private ownership, union leaders might consider saving jobs through the design and development of new products. Instead of viewing the impending shutdown as an unmitigated disaster, union leaders might regard the plant and its workers as material and human resources which, recombined in new and different ways, might yield new products and new jobs. The shop stewards combine of Lucas Aerospace in England has pioneered in this new strategy. While the unions at Lucas have been blocked by management from implementing plans to produce new products designed by their members, their program at Lucas has attracted wide attention and interest among leaders of management and unions in other companies (Centre for Alternative Industrial and Technical Systems 1979).

Two notes of caution regarding the general applicability of the Lucas example should be mentioned. First, in England engineers often belong to unions, and in fact, engineers played important roles in the Lucas project, working closely with blue-collar workers. To acquire engineering skills and experience, U.S. unions would have to co-opt engineers from the management staff or seek such cooperation from outside the company. Even in the Lucas case, the shop stewards combine did not go it alone. They established a jointly controlled research and development program with the Northeast London Polytechnic. Perhaps there is a U.S. university whose enginering school would be receptive to a jointly sponsored union-university program to create jobs.

Second, this strategy only offers long-term payoffs, and any project based on it would necessarily have to begin on a small scale. If a plant employing a thousand workers can avoid a shutdown through an employee buy-out and the plant can survive making the same products for the same markets, then it is possible to save hundreds of jobs even if the work force must be somewhat reduced. The development of new products for new markets is necessarily a slow process that can only employ a small number of workers in its early stages. But if it is impossible to continue producing the same products, then union leaders, seeking to save or create jobs, have only two options: cooperate with local government officials to attract a private company that will buy the plant and reemploy some of the workers or seek the support necessary for a program of new product development.

EMPLOYEE OWNERSHIP AND OTHER POLICY OPTIONS FOR MANAGEMENT

Employee ownership is not the only option management should consider in approaching the shutdown crisis. In a majority of cases, such an ownership transfer will not be practical. If the company seeks to meet its obligations for good corporate citizenship, however, management should consider employee ownership as one among several ways of meeting the needs of workers and community people.

Leaders of American business should recognize that other industrialized nations have gone far beyond the United States by law or custom in protecting job security of workers. In some European countries, it is practically impossible, except in the case of bankruptcy of the firm, to shut down a plant without first securing government approval. Japan has no such legislation, yet the norm of lifetime employment for a large part of the industrial labor force is so deeply engrained that for a well-established firm facing a downturn in demand for its products, layoffs or a plant closing are the last options to be considered by management.

International trends, combined with the recent experience of workers and union leaders, are bound to fuel continuing pressures for legislation to limit management rights to close plants and to impose on management other obligations designed to increase job security. There is little likelihood of such federal legislation in the near future, but as long as problems of worker job insecurity remain, prospects for such legislation will depend in part upon the ability of companies to devise their own solutions to the underlying problems.

Let us review experience in the recent past of management's handling of shutdown crises, beginning with a bad example. In 1975, a company announced the temporary closing of a plant employing four hundred fifty people. According to company officials, the plant would reopen within the next twelve months, as business conditions improved. About a year later, after workers had exhausted all of their unemployment insurance benefits, management announced that the plant would remain permanently closed. This change in plans was greeted by a storm of protest from union leaders, workers, and local public officials. Since the plant had long been the major employer in this small city, its closing provoked widespread community concern.

When they had failed to persuade management to reopen the plant, union leaders proposed a new idea: the company should sell the plant to the employees. Company officials declined to consider such a possibility and, when pressed to give a figure at which they might be willing to sell the plant, management quoted a sum based on the replacement cost of machines, some of which were twenty to thirty years old. Exasperated with this uncooperative stance, the union president told a company spokesman that management "owed it to this community" to either reopen the plant or to negotiate reasonable terms for its sale to the employees. The company spokesman responded, "In the forty years that this plant has been operating, the company has paid the highest wages and fringe benefits in this community and has been the biggest tax payer. The company does not owe anything to this community."

If the company spokesman had anticipated how this statement would look the next morning in the headlines of the local newspaper, no doubt he would have spoken in a less provocative fashion. Of course, the statement was legally correct, but the outrage it provoked among workers and community people focuses the issue. Does management indeed have no responsibilities to workers and the community beyond those specified by law? If managements generally take that position, they can hardly be surprised if workers continue to push for legislation imposing obligations upon management in the case of plant shutdowns.

In the spring of 1981, the business school of a major university arranged for chief executive officers of five of the country's largest companies to spend a day on campus to discuss the social responsibilities of business. During one of these sessions, a professor asked, "Do your companies have written policies about how you should handle plant shutdowns?" Four of the CEOs acknowledged that no such written policy existed in their companies. The fifth said that his company did indeed have such a policy statement, and he would be glad to send it to the professor. Two weeks later the professor received an apologetic letter from the executive stating that he distinctly remembered seeing such a policy statement at one time, but he had been unable to locate it! It is surprising and disappointing that these five major corporations were without firm policies on plant closings. It was as if management people preferred not to think about such an unpleasant event as the closing of a plant until a local situation forced them to face the problem, whereupon they necessarily had to improvise.

There are a number of positive actions that management might consider to help workers and community people ease the trauma of an impending shutdown. The most familiar of these strategies are based on the assumption that it is impossible to save the jobs and therefore the most management can do is provide assistance to workers as they seek to readjust to the economic disaster.

In some cases, union contracts call for severance pay based upon length of service. When no such contractual obligation exists, in some cases managements have nevertheless offered severance pay. In some cases, management has offered to employ laid off workers at another of its locations and has even been willing to pay travel expenses so that the worker can visit the new location and get some idea of how he and his family might adapt to this change. While such a voluntary offer is indeed generous, it can hardly repair the loss suffered by workers and the community. When workers have grown up in a community and have all their friends and many of their relatives there, the offer of a new job elsewhere is not an unmixed blessing. Furthermore, the move is likely to involve the loss of many years seniority as the transferred worker goes to the new plant as a new employee and thus almost always starts at a much lower rate than he or she was receiving before the shutdown. Finally, there is the potential financial loss in housing transactions. A home may represent the bulk of the worker's life savings. If the plant being shut down has been a major employer in a town or small city, the shutdown can so depress the real estate market that the worker can hardly give the home away. For reasons such as these workers have generally been extremely reluctant to move from a depressed community, even when they can anticipate better job opportunities elsewhere.

If management is willing to consider the possibility that the plant might continue in operation with the existing work force or some fraction of that work force, then the options for management are numerous although less familiar. In the first place, management can make a contribution simply by being willing to discuss seriously with worker representatives and community people the possibility of selling the plant to the employees. If management does sell, one of the first requests of its negotiating partners will be for the kinds of financial and operating information necessary to assess the possibilities of establishing a viable employee-owned firm. While management people are in general extremely reluctant to provide information they consider to be proprietary, the request does not have to be answered on a yes-or-no basis. Management might counter by asking representatives of the employees to specify which figures would be most important to them, and then, before providing that information, the two parties might seek to negotiate the terms under which the information might be provided with safeguards for confidentiality. These safeguards may be easier to establish if management cooperates with a consulting firm doing a feasibility study.

Who should own the land and buildings after the plant shuts down? In one case, after removing the machines from the plant, the company demolished buildings, some of which were in first-class condition and had been assessed at millions of dollars. The purpose of this destruction of valuable property was, of course, to remove the company's substantial property tax liability. In a contrasting case, when Diamond International Company announced the shutdown of its plant in Ogdensburg, New York, management deeded the plant to the city and also made a contribution of $22,000 to cover its maintenance for a period of time. The corporation hoped that the city would be able to use the physical facility as a base for attracting another employer, or for creating a firm to employ some or all of the displaced workers.

Some European firms have gone much farther than U.S. firms in alternative product development at locations where they propose to shut down plants (Clutterbuck 1980). In Japan, when the market imposes the need to reduce employment in any major industry or industrial area, management people work with unions and government to develop alternative employment opportunities. U.S. industrial leaders would find it worthwhile to review European and Japanese experience in this field.

IMPLICATIONS FOR FEDERAL GOVERNMENT POLICIES

Unfortunately, political arguments regarding the role of government tend to run to extremes: either the federal government is so clumsy and inefficient that it cannot do much of anything useful and the solution is to "get the government off our backs," or else the federal government is called upon to solve every important social and economic problem of the nation. Neither of these extreme views provides useful guidance for the future. The get-the-government-off-our-backs philosophy closes off opportunities for government intervention in problems that cannot be solved without some federal involvement, but at the same time even committed liberals are coming to recognize the limitations of programs that promise to do more things to and for more people.

Out of this clash of extreme views, a new participatory ideology is emerging. This ideology recognizes the inherent limitations of national government in running programs in local areas but also recognizes the great potential for federal leadership in stimulating and supporting locally based efforts. The Labor-Management Cooperation Act designed by Senator Jacob Javits and Representative Stanley N. Lundine is an important step in this direction. The act establishes funds, currently administered by the Federal Mediation and Conciliation Service, for grants to area labor-management committees and joint union-management cooperation programs in particular companies. Unfortunately, the Reagan administration has limited appropriations for this program to $500,000 for the 1982 fiscal year and is seeking to terminate support completely for the 1983 budget. There is a further important limitation: funds are provided only to those operating particular projects or programs. They are not available to researchers for studies designed to determine what makes the difference between success and failure and thus provide guidance in the development of more effective programs.

The importance of research may be illustrated by the recently negotiated contract between the Ford Motor Company and the UAW. The parties aimed toward the Japanese model of lifetime guaranteed jobs for a majority of company employees and have agreed to carry out this job security experiment in two or three major plants. The first plant chosen, in Livonia, Michigan, currently employs 3,150 unionized workers. An experiment of this significance calls for social research to document the process of implementing the plan, the problems that arise in this process, the way management and union leaders and workers cope with these problems, and the overall social and economic effects of the program. Since the Institute of Labor and Industrial Relations, jointly supported so far by the University of Michigan and Wayne State University, is recognized as one of the leading centers of industrial relations research and has had rich experience in studies in the automotive industry, one would assume that the research should be organized and directed from such an institute. Unfortunately, Michigan's budget has so drastically limited state government spending as to impose drastic cuts on university budgets. For the immediate future, it will be extremely difficult for the state of Michigan to provide adequate funds for such important social research. Furthermore, a strong claim can be made for federal financing for this type of study because it has nationwide implications. Unfortunately, the current administration has not only reduced drastically the funds available for social and economic research in the National Science Foundation and in the National Institute of Mental Health but has also slashed research funds in the U.S. Department of Labor, which would be the logical agency to support such research.

Beyond support for research, there are important financial needs in facilitating social and economic readjustment that the federal government can finance without becoming committed to pump funds into every depressed community and company. Consider, for example, the experience of the Economic Development Administration of the Department of Commerce, which since the mid-1960s has been the major government agency dealing with problems of distressed areas and companies. President Reagan and his advisers apparently embrace the social Darwinism doctrine, which dictates that government should not bail out a company whose existence is threatened by financial losses or support a community in a depressed condition. The theory is that a weak company should be allowed to die and a depressed community should not be more than minimally supported so that its citizens will be motivated to move elsewhere. It puts all faith for economic growth and expansion in employment in the growth of existing, profitable firms. Unfortunately, this doctrine has ruled out an objective study of the variety of programs that EDA has supported under mandates from Congress and the president. Such a study would undoubtedly indicate that some programs have simply postponed the inevitable death of a weak company or provided stopgap support that delayed a community's adjustment to inevitable changes. On the other hand, some of the programs have been highly cost-effective. For example, in the 1970s EDA provided more loan money to more cases of employee ownership than all other federal agencies combined, making possible the saving of thousands of jobs. To this date, the agency has been recovering all loan money that went into direct support of those projects.

A similar argument can be made for the evaluation and probable expansion of grant-loan programs carried out under EDA. In these, to support a company in difficulties or the saving of jobs through a transfer of ownership, EDA has not provided loans directly to the company but rather to a local economic development agency, which has then chaneled that money into the company. As long as it survives, the company pays the interest and principal on the loan to the local economic development agency rather than to the federal government. We can make no assessment of the overall value of that program, but the results of the two projects with which we have had experience have been so positive as to demand serious consideration. In order to save jobs in two Allegheny-Ludlum plants in New York State, EDA granted $6 million to the Chautauqua County Industrial Development Agency and $4 million to the Albany County Industrial Development Agency. The Chautauqua County IDA has been an important source of financial support for the training and other economic revitalization activities of JALMC. Furthermore, the local IDA has provided loan money essential to plant expansion and to retaining certain companies in that area that might otherwise relocate.

It was a $3 million grant by EDA to Black Hawk Economic Development Committee that enabled the county agency to make the loan that kept Rath Packing Company alive until it was possible to work out the transfer of majority ownership to the employees. It was then a $4.6 million Urban Development Action Grant to Waterloo that enabled the city to make the loan essential to the Rath employee ownership project. These two grant-loans not only saved more than fifteen hundred jobs in Waterloo (and more than one thousand jobs elsewhere) but strengthened the local tax base. As long as Rath continues paying principal and interest on these loans, the county agency and the city have revolving funds to use for local economic development projects. Officials of the Black Hawk Committee report that they have already used this revolving fund to provide loans to a dozen new businesses, as well as to support technical assistance to strengthen the labor-management cooperative process at Rath.

Such grant-loan programs are an important social invention: a creative combination of federal resources with local initiative and responsibility. Federal funds were essential in these cases. But if EDA (or HUD) had been responsible for monitoring the projects and collecting repayments, it is easy to imagine the bureaucratic delays and local-national frictions inevitably associated with development assistance by remote control that would have occurred. By granting money to local agencies, the federal agencies shifted initiative and responsibility to people with an intimate knowledge of local conditions and problems. Local people were then strongly motivated to administer an effective program because they recognized that the revolving fund so essential to local economic development can be maintained only if they themselves manage the funds and associated activities effectively.

Another potential model for federal assistance in industrial development is provided by the Tailored Clothing Technology Corporation (TCTC), an organization devised to aid companies and workers in the apparel industry to improve the productivity of U.S. plants faced with growing international competition. Here, the initiative was taken by the Amalgamated Clothing and Textile Workers of America, which secured the cooperation of three of the leading companies in the field. To establish and finance the corporation for a two- to three-year period, the union and the companies made equal annual contributions totaling $250,000, and the U.S. Department of Commerce matched these funds. The union and the companies have equal representation on the board of directors of TCTC.

In the past, companies in the clothing industry have tried to improve productivity by developing machines that increase the speed of production operations. Union officials pointed out that actual production work accounted for only about 25 percent of total labor time, with the remaining 75 percent being devoted to materials handling. This led to a decision to concentrate technological research and development on the creation of a machine to speed up the materials handling operations. The Tailored Clothing Technology Corporation contracted with Draper Laboratories for this work. At this writing, a prototype of the machine is being tested, and the parties hope to begin the process of introducing the machine into the apparel plants within the next twelve to eighteen months. The machine is to be patented by TCTC, and the parties have agreed to give U.S. firms the first opportunity to manufacture it, thus contributing to the growth of the U.S. machine tool industry.

We can also look for guidance to other nations. Consider the case of Japan, a nation with a dynamic private economy but one in which the government plays an exceedingly important role in stimulating and guiding the economy and in assisting companies in working out adjustments to changes in demand for their products. Currently, Japan is experiencing a major readjustment in the aluminum industry. Since aluminum smelting requires enormous amounts of energy, which is much more costly in Japan than in many other nations, it has become apparent that the aluminum companies can no longer sustain lifetime employment within their smelting operations. Currently, a number of the smelting facilities are gradually being phased out while unions and management work out plans to shift workers from smelting into fabrication plants. The Japanese government is a major actor in this process, drawing on research from the Japan Institute of Labor and involving technical and financial assistance from the Ministry of International Trade and Industry and the Ministry of Finance. It is too early to offer definitive results, since the process is still in the early stages, but the important point is that the government is intimately involved in the process of change, seeking to help support employment of workers and the economic viability of the companies.

Closer to home is the Canadian Manpower Consultative Service, which, on a voluntary basis, works with companies and unions on projects designed to facilitate adjustments of human resources to changes in technology and market conditions (Batt 1982). Each project is developed from a manpower assessment incentive agreement, which brings the company, the workers, and their union together with the Federal Ministry of Employment and Immigration and the Provincial Ministry of Labor. The agreement establishes a manpower adjustment committee with equal representation of management and workers, and a chairperson from outside the company is selected jointly by the parties. One official from the federal government and one from the provincial government act as consultants. The committee studies the adjustment problems and works out plans for what management, the union, and government agencies can do to meet the problems. The government does not impose any solutions but offers a social process, technical assistance, and financial incentives to help the parties arrive at mutually satisfactory solutions.

We provide these necessarily brief descriptions of foreign programs not suggesting that any foreign model should be simply transplanted into the United States, but to point out the unusual situation of U.S. industry: at the present time the United States appears to be the only industrialized nation that has no overall policies guiding government involvement in area, industry, and company economic and social readjustment programs—unless leaving all these problems to the private sector can be considered a policy. Elements of such a policy had been developing within EDA, but the Reagan administration has been trying to abolish that agency. Such an interesting case as government cooperation with management and labor in the apparel industry is an isolated instance and hardly constitutes government policy. Government's intervention to save Chrysler Corporation from bankruptcy was a very important case, but that agreement among company, union, banks, and government was hammered out through hectic weeks of maneuvering in the halls of Congress. No one would argue that the Chrysler case represents a model of how government economic readjustment and development decisions should be made.

The choice of solutions is not between the federal government assuming responsibility for supporting every depressed industry or community or the government doing nothing. The problem requires finding an American solution in which the government develops policies for selective intervention with technical assistance and money in support of strongly based management, union, and local community efforts to solve industry or area problems. Legislation to restructure and expand government's economic and industrial development activities is needed. While it is not possible to go into any details here regarding the general provisions needed, it will be worthwhile to turn to the specific legislative needs to promote employee ownership, since this is the area in which we have substantial experience.

LEGISLATION SUPPORTING EMPLOYEE OWNERSHIP

Employee ownership is compatible with democratic values deeply embedded in American culture. When a national sample was surveyed in 1975 on the question as to whether respondents would prefer to work in a firm owned by stockholders outside of the firm, by government, or by employees, 66 percent chose employee ownership. Furthermore, employee ownership transcends traditional political ideologies and cleavages, having strong support both on the right and on the left. People continue to try to identify the idea with traditional ideological categories, but it simply does not fit. Conservatives are inclined to call employee ownership "people's capitalism," or "popular capitalism," whereas liberals and radicals attach the label of "democratic socialism." Such terms are misleading. For a century, capitalism has meant to most people a system in which ownership is limited to an individual or a small group of individuals running a company or to a large number of stockholders, few if any of whom work for the company. Socialism has meant government ownership and control of the means of production. The use of the adjective democratic is not going to erase the well-established meaning of socialism in the minds of most people. It seems to us that, at least in instances where worker-owners have the right to vote, the most appropriate political label is *economic democracy*. While it is not up to us to attach a political label to the phenomenon, this one might eliminate the confusions that inevitably arise when employee ownership is forced into one or another traditional political category.

Much of the trend toward employee ownership should be attributed to Louis Kelso, lawyer and investment banker, who developed an unorthodox two-value theory of economic development. Pointing to the high level of concentration of corporation ownership in the hands of a very small percentage of the population, he argued that the American system of private enterprise was bound to run into increasing difficulties as long as workers depended for their income entirely upon wages. He saw the inclusion of workers as co-owners of firms in which they worked as a means of increasing their motivation. Thus productivity would be enhanced and labor-management conflict reduced, while at the same time workers'. adherence to the current economic system would be strengthened.

Kelso wanted workers simply to share in ownership and management to be left strictly to professional managers. Furthermore, the theory simply visualized affecting workers' attitudes and motivations through providing them with a share in ownership in existing profitable companies. At the time he and Mortimer Adler published *The Capitalist Manifesto* (1961), Kelso had no thought of applying his notions to employee purchase of plants being shut down.

Kelso interested Senator Russell Long in his ideas, and this led to the enactment of the first ESOP legislation in 1974. The act allowed companies to set up employee stock ownership trusts and to use up to 15 percent of payroll to buy stock in the company for employees. The main incentive for management at this time was facilitation in raising capital.

By 1977, EDA had used the ESOP instrument as a means of financing the purchase of several plants about to be closed by employers. Observing both the potentials and the problems of saving jobs through employee or employee-community purchase of the plant, we began work on a public policy project that led to the introduction in the House of Representatives of the Voluntary Job Preservation and Community Stabilization Act. The impetus for this bill emerged from two aspects of our field observations. Although several well-publicized cases of job saving through employee ownership had already taken place with government financial support, EDA, the agency most involved in this activity, had established no policies for dealing with potential employee ownership cases and was dealing with each potential shutdown case by case, providing loans and technical assistance for employee ownership only when all other options seemed doomed to failure. Furthermore, because Congress mandated new priorities for EDA without providing additional funds, the possibility for EDA action in support of employee ownership was declining. This suggested that the potential for job saving through employee ownership could be exploited by government only if EDA received additional funds and a mandate to develop policy and program for employee ownership.

The other research observation shaping this bill was that, in the emergency of an impending plant shutdown, employees were inclined to think only of the immediate task of saving the jobs and therefore would accept whatever ownership arrangement was proposed to them. Under these circumstances, it was natural to accept a traditional stock ownership arrangement, which, as we have already noted, inevitably leads to the loss of employee ownership and control in the long run. The representatives introducing the bill did not believe it appropriate for the federal government to tell employees what form of organization and control they should adopt, but settled instead upon the "informed choice" principle. As written into the bill, before the organizing group receives any federal assistance, they must "Certify to the Secretary [of Commerce] that the form of ownership and control . . . has been adopted by members of the organization after full consideration and deliberation of all options relating to the form of ownership and control available under the laws of the State in which the concern is located. . . ."

In this research-legislation project, Whyte took primary responsibility for feeding in information and ideas gained from research at Cornell and elsewhere, and Joseph Blasi, director of the Project for Kibbutz Studies at Harvard University, provided the chief link between the academic world and Congress. At the time Blasi was working with Representative Peter H. Kostmayer of Pennsylvania. Representatives Matthew F. McHugh and Stanley N. Lundine, both of New York, joined with Kostmayer in introducing the Voluntary Job Preservation and Community Stabiliza-

tion Act to the House of Representatives March 1, 1978. Among
the many thousands of bills introduced each year in the House of
Representatives, a bill cosponsored by three junior congressmen
will not be taken seriously unless they can persuade a large number
of their colleagues to commit themselves as cosponsors of the bill.
The bill attracted serious attention among staff members and legis-
lators in both houses. When the Ninety-fifth Congress adjourned
in October 1978, approximately one out of every six members of
the House had signed on as cosponsors.

Corey Rosen, then a staff member to the Senate Select Committee on Small Business, took a special interest in this initial bill
and worked closely with Senators Gaylord Nelson and Donald
Stewart in drafting the Small Business Employee Ownership Act,
which became law in July 1980. Although narrower in scope than
the Voluntary Job Preservation and Community Stabilization Act,
the Small Business Employee Ownership Act is exceedingly important in directing the Small Business Administration to cease
discriminating against actual or potential employee-owned firms in
their loan and loan guarantee policies. Up to this time Small Business Administration policy makers had been reluctant to support
any form of employee ownership and furthermore had taken the
legalistic position that an employee stock ownership trust is not a
small business and therefore is not eligible for SBA loans or loan
guarantees. Since the ESOP appeared to be the most useful instrument for employee purchase of a firm threatening to go out of
business, this interpretation represented a serious obstacle to employee ownership.

A 1980 Small Business Administration task force on small
business continuity focused attention on a problem generally ig-
nored by economists: how to facilitate the transfer of ownership of
a profitable small firm to those able to maintain a viable business
when the original entrepreneur-owners retire or die. Under existing legislation, if the owners sell the firm to a large company in
exchange for stock, they escape the capital gains tax they would
have to pay if they sold to employees or to a group of private
investors. The task force recommended that this discrimination in
favor of big business be eliminated by treating sale to an employee
ownership stock trust the same as to a corporation. The task force

also proposed that the heirs to the owner of a successful small business be relieved of estate taxes on that business by having the firm's ESOP assume responsibility for that tax liability.

As Congress increasingly recognizes the problem of continuity of successful small businesses and the importance of small business for job creation and economic growth, we can expect passage of such supporting legislation in the near future. Such legislation may well make small business the sector of most rapid growth of employee ownership.

Senator Russell Long continues to work on measures in support of employee ownership. At this writing, he is considering possible use of pension funds to provide collateral for stock purchased for an ESOP. He is also suggesting that dividends on employee-owned stock be treated like wages and therefore be exempt from taxation on company profits (Long 1982).

The National Development Investment Act (H.R. 6100) introduced in 1982 contains clauses designed to support employee ownership, especially as a means of avoiding a plant shutdown. The bill would authorize EDA to support feasibility studies and to assist with financing in the purchase of a plant or company. Reporting on this bill, the House Committee on Public Works and Transportation accurately reflects research findings in this field:

> The availability of technical assistance will often be critical to the success of an employee-ownership venture. The Committee particularly recognizes the need for assistance in organizational redesign. The experiences of employee-owned firms suggest that tensions may arise if employee-owners are not given input in the management of their own business. Two provisions in this bill are intended to forestall such conflicts. First, voting rights must accompany stock which is allocated to employees under any assisted plan. In addition, any assisted business is required to conduct periodic reviews of employees' role in the management of that business.

At present, many proponents of economic democracy have mixed reactions to ESOPs. Clearly, the recent surge in employee ownership has been facilitated by ESOPs, and the tax and other financial advantages of the ESOP are likely to stimulate further growth. Since the ESOP was not originally designed to foster economic democracy, it remains to be seen to what extent it can be used to achieve this goal.

IMPLICATIONS FOR STATE AND LOCAL GOVERNMENTS

The unproductive nature of efforts to attract big companies into a state or a community suggests that the often considerable resources devoted to such programs could be reduced with little sacrifice by the citizens of the state. Funds could then be shifted into the development of technical assistance for working with companies, unions, and interested local people in helping economic transitions, stimulating and partially supporting local area labor-management committees, cushioning the effects of layoffs and plant shutdowns, and developing new jobs and new companies. Furthermore, any state has some millions of dollars to be allocated to economic development projects. These funds can more effectively spent if officials give special attention to local projects involving high degrees of participation by management and union leaders and community people.

In 1979 Michigan became the first state to enact employee ownership legislation, but at that point the state department of labor was directed to provide technical assistance for such projects, without the appropriation of any additional state funds. In 1982 Michigan enacted an Economic Development Authority Act, providing the first state authority for financing employee ownership:

> [under] this Act, an economic development authority is established and directed to "fund at least five industrial facilities conversion projects" each year. The Act provides a priority for employee buyout efforts.
> Funding comes from a revolving loan fund. Loan maximums are $1,000,000 unless two-thirds of the Authority's board votes otherwise. The law requires that employees have full voting rights on all allocated and unallocated shares (Rosen 1982).

At this writing, eight other states have followed Michigan's lead in legislating programs to support employee ownership. They are California, Minnesota, Illinois, Ohio, Massachusetts, New Jersey, Delaware, and Maryland. While the laws vary in detail, all of them at least require a state agency to provide information about employee ownership and to provide some technical assistance to organizations seeking to establish this this form of ownership. The Massachusetts law changes preexisting legislation on cooperatives so as to facilitate the growth of worker cooperatives. The still rapidly growing political interest suggests that many more states will enact laws supporting employee ownership and worker cooperatives before the end of the 1980s.

BEYOND CURRENT IDEOLOGIES

Those who wish to contribute to the economic and social revitalization of America must learn to place particular projects and plans within an emerging development strategy. The ideology of free enterprise would have us believe that initiatives for business and industrial development must be left strictly to the private sector. At the other extreme are those who see progress in terms of having the national government do more things for and to people. Neither ideology will provide useful guidance for the America of the 1980s and beyond.

The revitalization of America must come through strengthening local initiatives and responsibilities. Employee ownership and labor-management cooperation can play significant roles in this process. These initiatives, however, cannot yield their potential benefits without financial support and technical assistance from the national and state governments. Instead of simply seeking to regulate activities, government can stimulate and support locally based initiatives. Governments can help to empower people to make better use of the material and human resources in their communities.

References

Aldrich, Howard, and Stern, Robert N.
   1983   "Resource Mobilization and the Creation of U.S. Producer
           Cooperatives, 1835–1935." *Economic and Industrial Democracy*
           (forthcoming).
Batt, William L., Jr.
   1982   "Plant Closings: An Improved Approach." *County Employ-
           ment Reporter*, August.
Birch, David
   1979   *The Job Generation Process*. Washington, D.C.: Economic De-
           velopment Administration.
Blondman, Mark
   1978   "The Development of Community Level Labor-Manage-
           ment Committees." Master's thesis, Cornell University.
Bluestone, Barry, and Harrison, Bennett
   1982   *The Deindustrialization of America: Plant Closings, Community
           Abandonment, and the Dismantling of Basic Industry*. New
           York: Basic Books.
Carey, Hugh L.
   1981   *The New York State Economy in the 1980s: A Program for Eco-
           nomic Growth*.

Centre for Alternative Industrial and Technological Systems
    1979   *Lucas Aerospace: Turning Industrial Decline into Expansion*. London: Northeast London Polytechnic.
Clutterbuck, David
    1980   "Keeping Workers off the Scrap Heap." *International Management* (June): 12–20.
Cole, Robert
    1979   *Work Mobility and Participation: A Comparative Study of American and Japanese Industry*. Berkeley: University of California Press.
Cox, Donald
    1979   Testimony before Senate Select Committee on Small Business on S. 388, the Small Business Employee Ownership Act, Ninety-sixth Congress, 1st Session, Feb. 27, 1979.
Ellerman, David
    1980   "What Is a Worker Cooperative?" Somerville, Mass.: Industrial Cooperative Association.
    1982   "Notes on the Co-op/ESOP Debate." Somerville, Mass.: Industrial Cooperative Association.
Foltman, Felician
    1976   "Labor-Management Cooperation at the Community Level: How to Start up and Maintain Community Level and Labor-Management Committees." Unpublished manuscript, New York State School of Industrial and Labor Relations, Cornell University.
Greenberg, Edward
    1981   "Industrial Self-Management and Political Attitudes." *American Political Science Review* 75, 1 (March).
    1982   "Producers Cooperatives and Democratic Theory." In *Industrial Democracy*, edited by Henry Levin. Palo Alto, Calif.: Center for Economic Studies.
Gutiérrez-Johnson, Ana
    1982   "Economic Democracy in Action: The Mondragón Cooperative Complex." Ph.D. diss., Cornell University.
Gutiérrez-Johnson, Ana, and Whyte, William Foote
            "The Mondragón System of Worker Production Cooperatives." *Industrial and Labor Relations Review* 31, 1 (October 1977):18–30.
Hammer, Tove Helland, and Stern, Robert N.
    1980   "Employee Ownership: Implications for the Organizational Distribution of Power." *Academy of Management Journal* 23, 1 (March).
JALMC
    1974   *Three Productive Years*. Jamestown, N.Y.

Keidel, Robert W.
    1981a   *How to Form an In-Plant Labor-Management Committee.* Philadelphia: Philadelphia Area Labor-Management Committee.
    1981b   "Theme Appreciation as a Construct for Organizational Change." *Management Science* 27, 11 (November).
Kelly, Ed, and Webb, Lee
    1979   *Plant Closings: Resources for Public Officials and Trade Unionists.* Washington, D.C.: Conference on Alternative State and Local Policies.
Kelso, Louis, and Adler, Mortimer
    1961   *The Capitalist Manifesto.* New York: Random House.
Long, Russell
    1982   "Worker Ownership: Spreading Free Enterprise." *Economic Democracy* 4, 2 (Summer).
Lundine, Stanley
    1982   "The Jamestown Experience: A Case Study in Labor-Management Cooperation." In *Managing Innovation: The Social Dimensions of Creativity, Invention, and Technology,* edited by Sven B. Lundstedt and E. William Colglazier, Jr. New York: Pergamon Press.
Meek, Christopher
    1983   "Labor-Management Cooperation and Economic-Revitalization: The Story of the Growth and Development of the Jamestown Area Labor-Management Committee." Ph.D. diss., Cornell University.
O'Leary, J.
    1974   *Industrial Development in New York State.* Albany, N.Y.: Legislative Commission Expenditure Review.
Rosen, Corey
    1982a   "Michigan Passes Employee Ownership Bill," *Employee Ownership* 2, 1 (National Center for Employee Ownership, Arlington, Va.).
    1982b   "Union Conference a Great Success." *Employee Ownership* (March).
Servan-Schreiber, Jean-Jacques
    1968   *The American Challenge.* New York: Harper & Bros.
Simmons, John
    1982   "Workers Have Brains Too: An Interview with Irving Bluestone." *Workplace Democracy* 9:4.
Smith, James
    1982   "The Labor Movement and Worker Ownership." *The Social Report* (December). Chestnut Hill, Mass.: Program in Social Economy and Social Policy, Boston College.

Sokoloff, Gail Lauren
    1982   "The Creation of an Employee Owned Firm." Honors the-
            sis, Department of Sociology, Harvard University.
Stern, Robert N., and Hammer, Tove Helland
    1978   "Buying Your Job: Factors Affecting the Success or Failure
            of Employee Acquisition Attempts." *Human Relations* 31:
            1101–17.
Stern, Robert N., and O'Brien, Rae Ann
    1977   "National Unions and Employee Ownership." Unpub-
            lished.
Strauss, George
    1955   "Group Dynamics and Intergroup Relations." Chapter 10 in
            Money and Motivation by William F. Whyte et al. New York:
            Harper & Bros.
Trist, Eric; Susman, G. I.; and Brown, G. R.
    1977   "An Experiment in Autonomous Working in an American
            Underground Coal Mine." *Human Relations* 30, 3: 201–36.
Whyte, William F.
    1950   *Leadership and Group Participation.* Ithaca, N.Y.: New York
            State School of Industrial and Labor Relations, Cornell
            University.

Sources of Information and Technical Assistance

Center for Community Self-Help
P.O. Box 3259
West Durham, NC 27705
Assistance in employee ownership projects

ESOP Association of America
1725 DeSales St., NW, Suite 400
Washington, DC 20036
Directed primarily to companies with established ESOPs. Annual conference, regional meetings, bulletins on ESOP news, references to information sources

Grey Areas
132 South Bonsall St.
Philadelphia, PA 19103
Educational services and technical assistance

Industrial Cooperative Association
249 Elm St.
Somerville, MA 02144
Educational services and technical assistance

National Center for Employee Ownership
    1611 So. Walter Reed Drive, No. 109
    Arlington, VA 22204
    Bulletin, research report series, conferences, and consultant referral by region

Center for New Economic Development
    109 Minna St., Suite 296
    San Francisco, CA 94105
    Educational services and technical assistance

Philadelphia Area Cooperative Enterprises (PACE)
    1321 Arch St., 8th Floor
    Philadelphia, PA 19107
    Educational services and technical assistance

UNIVERSITY RESOURCES

Department of Organizational Behavior
    Warner Woodworth
    Brigham Young University
    Provo, UT 84602

Center for Kibbutz Studies
    Joseph Blasi, Director
    Vanserg Hall
    Harvard University
    Cambridge, MA 02138

New Systems of Work and Participation Program
    William F. Whyte, Director
    368 Ives Hall
    Cornell University
    Ithaca, NY 14853

Program on Employee Participation and Enterprise Planning
    Donald Kane, Peter Lazes, William F. Whyte, codirectors
    Conference Center
    New York State School of Industrial and Labor Relations
    Cornell University
    Ithaca, NY 14853

Program in Social Economy and Social Policy
    Severyn Bruyn, Director
    Department of Sociology
    Boston College
    Chestnut Hill, MA 02167

Index